A LEMON GROWS IN QUEENS

*Stories from an
Italian-American Girl
Navigating Life in Chaos*

by Darlene Fusco Weinbrenner

Edited by Lil Barcaski

Published by: GWN Publishing
www.GWNPublishing.com

Cover Design: Kristina Conatser

ISBN: 978-1-959608-72-1

DEDICATION

This book is dedicated to my husband John, my daughter, Jacquelyn, my son, John, and my brother, Joseph. My heart is divided into four equal parts.

"My heart will always remember when I was drowning, the ones who held their hand out to pull me from the deep and the ones who pretended not to see a thing."

-Stephanie Bennett-Henry

TABLE OF CONTENTS

FOREWORD

For as long as I can remember, I've always loved writing. When I was a child, I would write short stories. Later, in my teenage years, my friend and I would spend afternoons writing, then switch and read each other's stories. Then, in my late teens, I spent three years in a confusing depression. I barely ate and couldn't sleep. When morning came, I didn't want to wake up. When it was time for bed, I didn't want to sleep.

I found a job in my neighborhood in a shoe store, and working slowly got me out of depression. It kept me busy and my mind on other things. I continued writing and eventually published a book for preteens called, *Hannah, Mable, and the Moving Van*.

This memoir is for my family and anyone who wants to understand what it's like to grow up in an Italian-American family, filled with love and laughter, pain and sorrow, being bullied and getting a cancer diagnosis. It will always be etched in who I am.

My memoir is written in short stories about growing up in Corona, Queens and moving to Long Island at the age of fifteen. There, I was assaulted, got married and gave birth to two of my most precious blessings, my children. I was also confronted with breast cancer, various surgeries, a superstorm, a fire, my husband's heart attacks, and a myriad of other health issues. A fire took us from our comfort zone for a year to the day, all while becoming the caregiver for both of my parents—so, yes, I've lived through the ups and downs, like all of us have.

Some have had more downs than others, but like they say, what doesn't kill us makes us stronger. Still, I'm an optimist, and I know having hope is better than giving up.

THE SS DANTE ALIGHIERI

The SS Dante Alighieri pulled from its port in Naples, Italy, in 1920. It carried aboard my great-grandmother, Rafaela, and her four youngest children, one of whom was my maternal grandmother, Laura. She was ten years old.

Years later, her father, my great-grandfather, would join them.

The three-thousand-mile journey to America was a frightening, daunting trip. The voyage took a little over two months. There was little comfort in the cramped quarters they slept in. The weather was often unpredictable, with strong winds and heavy rain. There was little to eat. Rats and lice ran rampant. Yet despite the many discomforts—overcrowding, dampness, and the ever-present putrid odor of urine mixed with salt—they were excited to land on American soil.

A new life lie ahead in a new country with half of their hearts left behind.

As they approached Ellis Island, there was much to be in awe of. The Statue of Liberty stood tall and welcoming. She was a mighty sight, and the skyscrapers accompanying her along the horizon gave a sense of newness and excitement. A foreign county with so much yet to be explored.

When they eventually reached their destination, a sense of urgency filled the air like electricity. It was an unspoken fact that they faced a strict inspection before being allowed to continue on. There was an anxiousness forthcoming. No one was certain they would pass the mental and physical inspections, and to be turned away would mean returning to Italy. Another trip that would take up to three months would be soul crushing.

Once they disembarked, the women and children were called to one side, the men to the other. This separation was routine regulation, and the inspectors worked by the book. Many were intimidated by the inspectors, who offered no leniency or trace of warmth—they were quite miserable.

The Italians called Ellis Island, "Isola Della Lacrime," or the "Island of Tears," because of the impending fear that some of their family members could be turned away. Though it was, in fact, only a small two percent that were.

The SS Dante Alighieri

They were checked for diseases of the eyes, ears, mouth, and nose and monitored closely, including an inspection of their mental state if someone looked odd, or off in some way. Eighty percent of the immigrants passed, while the other twenty percent were held for further questioning, and some were sent to the on-site hospital. A small percentage failed and were sent back home without their loved ones.

If it was a minor, one parent was chosen to accompany their child, leaving the family broken and separated.

Rafaela, my great-grandmother, came to America to help her son who had recently lost his wife. Rafaela and her children settled in Brooklyn with him and his now motherless children. My future grandmother, Laura, and her sisters, Victoria and Julia, took jobs in a sewing factory when they reached the age where they were able to work and contribute to the family.

They eventually moved to Manhattan and lived on 9th Avenue and 42nd Street, above a fish market and grocery store. As a small child, I would visit them. I can still smell the musty fish and hear the commotion in the streets. I have memories of visiting grandma's brother, Uncle Jerry and his wife, Connie, in that same apartment building.

I recall the swishing sounds of buses going by, the release of the brakes when they took off again, the acrid odor emanating from below, and the intermittent honking car horns. There was a Chock Full of Nuts Cafe on the corner that lit up the entire street. It was exciting to be in a bustling environment.

My mother, Giovanna, later dubbed Joan, was the firstborn to my grandparents and later a son came along, my mother's brother, who was named Joseph. My mother had a real talent for singing from an early age. She loved to sing, and my Grandpa Angelo thought she should share this with the world. He took mom to the Wally Jackson Studio to sing on a radio show in the late 1940's. One of the other children that was signed up to sing was Connie Francis who later became an Italian singing icon.

Mom might have gone far in her singing career if she hadn't met my dad. She chose her love for him and was happy to become his wife, learning that she wanted that more than a singing career. They fell head over heels in love, and she decided to give up singing. In those days, women very rarely had a career as well as being wife and mother.

Dad gave her an engagement ring two weeks after they met. He was fresh out of the army and was afraid he'd lose her if he didn't act fast. He told my grandparents that he'd step away if they told him no, but they embraced him into their lives.

THE FUSCO CLAN - MY FATHER'S FAMILY

"Hi, Carl. How's the family?"the shouts from friends on the streets of his Bronx neighborhood would call out to my dad. Johnny, Rosario, Mario, Luca, Louie, Joey, Danny, and Linda—it almost sounded like a song from saying it throughout the years. Nine kids trying to get by, as my paternal Grandmother, Tina, grappled with raising them. I remember how gentle and sweet she was. She wore a quiet, tender smile. Her hair was as white as the clouds, and her eyes were the warmest hues of baby blue. She was short in stature and wore mostly dresses with low heels and no stockings. The struggle to make ends meet, along with having nine children, did not make her nurture or love any one of them less than the other. She had her hands full raising them, virtually by herself. Eight boys, each rougher and tougher than the next. And one tiny, angelic little girl, Linda. She had sixteen eyeballs set on overprotecting her—their little porcelain doll. And they did just that.

Once, on a walk home after helping his dad sell fruit from his wagon, my dad, was handed a flyer. He brought it inside and dropped it on the kitchen table. When Grandma Tina read it, she was intrigued. Something in the writing resonated with her in a deeply profound way.

That flyer changed everything for her.

She became a Jehovah's Witness. No longer Catholic, she devoted her life, and many of her encounters, attempting to convert anyone who would listen. That greatly upset my mother. She would demand my dad ask her to stop talking to us children about it.

He would say, "Mom, you're confusing the kids."

"Okay, Carlo," she would reply, but she never actually stopped.

After a time, we would learn to turn a deaf ear to it. Some of her sons eventually converted and would preach when they could. It was a balance of trying not to be rude and rejecting conversation at all costs.

We very rarely got together, but I always loved them, and each of my uncles had a sweetness to them that I believe came from Grandma Tina.

I wish I'd spent more time with her and gotten to know my uncles and their families better.

CORONA

My parents married in 1953 and started a family soon after they wed. My sister, Joann, was born while they lived with my grandparents on 9th Avenue to save money. Two years later, they bought a four-family house – with four separate apartments – in Corona, Queens. Dad was good with money and saved while in the army. When they married, he gave my mom a bank book and told her to save every payday, no matter the amount. Five dollars here and there added up. And each pay period, he asked to see the bank book, happy the numbers kept rising.

They had my brother, Carlo, and then I came along another two and a half years later. With a nice six-year break for mom, my brother Joe was born.

Soon after moving to Corona, my grandparents moved into the house taking the ground floor, back apartment. Eventually my Aunt Julia took the upstairs, back apartment with her husband, Jack. The only tenant not related to us was Rose, who lived there before we did, with her husband, Phil. I guess they came with the house! They resided on the ground floor, front apartment. Unluckily, for Rose, the six of us lived right over her head.

Summers spent in Corona had us kids playing outside all day. Mom would sit on the stoop and chat with neighbors before eventually going upstairs to cook dinner. We rarely ate out with the occasional stop at a burger joint on the way home from the beach. She made meals that she learned to cook from my grandmother, usually consisting of chicken cutlets, pasta fagioli, spaghetti with meatballs, that we had every Sunday in my grandmother's tiny apartment downstairs, and once in a while, she made London broil. When she served that, my brother

Carlo accused her of making us eat horse meat. "What's wrong with you, would I give you horse meat?" She'd say with a laugh. We could eat in the living room and watch TV if we wanted to. That was the only time we had the TV to ourselves.

In those days, TVs didn't come with remote controls— but he had me and my siblings for that. All four of us took turns standing by the bulky, bulbously backed screen to change the channels at his command.

Far left, maternal grandfather, Angelo, Uncle Joe (mom's brother), my mother, my father, my maternal grandmother, Laura, my sister, Joann. Bottom row, my brother Carlo, my brother Joseph being held, and me in the front.

DAD

Dad was raised in a world where he had to be tough. The eldest of eight siblings, 'The Fusco Boys' were a bunch to be reckoned with on the streets of the Bronx. They had a reputation that most wouldn't challenge. "The Baldies" were, in a sense, their 'gang' name. I am not sure what all that entailed, as I was not privy to that information.

"Only the strong survive," was dad's mantra.

I believe his saving grace was going into the army at nineteen. It taught him discipline, teamwork, how to manage money, and many additional life skills he would have otherwise not learned.

Dad had a tendency to fly off the handle and that made mom nervous. She had no idea if it would escalate at any given time. She kept her mouth shut and let him go off on a tangent. At least, most of the time his anger wasn't towards any of us, just someone else he encountered.

Once when we were in the car, a bus cut in front of him. At a red light, he got out and banged on the back of the bus with his fists. The passengers were looking at him as if he were a lunatic, and from our view, he looked like one.

Despite his temper, he had a sense of humor and could tell a good joke or two. People would say to mom, "You must laugh all day."

She'd roll her eyes and reply, "Yeah, all day!"

He was handsome and charming, and although he only went to third grade, he was street smart and taught himself to read. He spoke some Italian, and so did mom, occasionally going between it and English when they felt the need.

Mom at her wedding with my dad's mother (Joan's mother in law).

Grandma Laura and my dad, Carlo

Mom was the softness dad needed. Especially for what was to come—a family.

Dad was a hard worker and a good provider, but I barely remember having any real conversation with him in my childhood although I do remember when my brother Joe was born, and he took me aside and said, "You are no longer the baby." He was trying to comfort me, but I couldn't understand why.

It didn't dawn on me that I was no longer the center of their world because I never felt like I was to begin with. His birth never felt like an intrusion; I loved him very much.

Dad was a roofer, and worked hard, even in the sweltering heat and the coldest of winter days. Rain, however, was his enemy. On those days, he couldn't work. And no work meant no pay. Those were the hardest for him. He was like a fish out of water if he couldn't keep himself busy or clown around with his co-workers all day.

Being of Italian descent, his skin was an olive complexion and his was rough to the touch. The sun was relentless and gave him a light bronze hue. He was also short, dark and hairy. We teased him about the fur coat he wore all year round!

At the end of each day, he knew he'd be coming home to a hot meal and a comfy sofa. On some occasions, he'd lie on the floor and play games with us. We'd take turns standing on the palms of his hands and hovering over him while he pushed us up. He would stand on his feet and tell us to grab a fistful of his hair and not to let go. Then he'd lift his head up as far as he could. I was always afraid of hurting him, but he told me it made his hair stronger. He would also do pushups with one or two of us on his back.

My paternal Grandfather, Rosario.

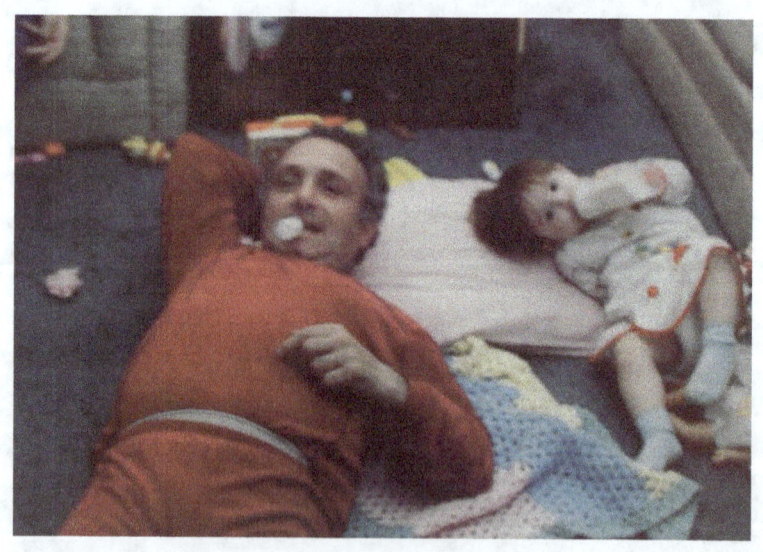

My dad Carlo and Jacquelyn, best friends.

Dad had a stash of candy hidden in the back of his closet, and when we wanted a piece of bubble gum, he would do 'tricks' and pull it out of thin air or do some 'fancy' hand gestures, and voila—gum would appear to have come out of one of his ears. I admit, it was a silly ritual we'd have to go through. Mom was worse, though. She kept a pack of spearmint gum in her purse. She would oblige without the magic, but she would tear a strip in half so what we got was pointless.

A half strip of gum or a ritual with second-rate magic tricks? We'd pick the magic tricks.

I never knew much about my dad's side of the family. We visited Grandma Tina on occasion, which I found to be uncomfortable and sad. Uncomfortable because they lived in a tiny apartment with little furniture. Sad because they lived in extreme poverty.

On one visit to see grandma, dad left mom and us kids there and went to meet his friends at a local bar. It was getting late, and when he didn't return, my brother Carlo went to see if he could find him. He must have been about twelve years old.

Just thinking of my son wandering around at night, going from bar to bar to find his father is mind blowing.

Eventually, to our surprise, he found him. Intoxicated of course.

After some time, dad came back, and Grandma Tina made black coffee to sober him up. Mom put us to bed in the other room—the only other room in the apartment. It had two bunk beds and a considerable number of cockroaches. They hide in the light, so when mom flipped the switch in the bedroom, they scattered away until it went dark again.

Not having ever seen a cockroach before, I jumped up to protest but was told to lie down and be quiet. I was near hysterics internally, but dared not make a sound, even when something would crawl over me.

I overheard my mother calling home to speak with her own mother, who already lived downstairs from us in Corona. She'd be worried if we didn't get back early. Mom told her we were having such a good time, we'd be late. She was worried grandma would make judgments about dad, so she lied instead.

It seemed like forever before dad began to feel better and was sober enough to drive us from the Bronx to Queens. It was after midnight as we headed down the many flights of steps, wishing there was an elevator. My mother kept asking if he was okay to drive, as he bounced from the wall to the railing while descending. He said he was fine, but that didn't stop Carlo and Joann from volunteering to drive instead. In the end, though, dad got us home safe and sound, and we never mentioned anything to grandma.

Growing up in Queens, the summers were long and stifling hot. On most weekends, we'd pile into the car and head to Long Beach to cool off at the ocean. Mom made sandwiches and packed towels. She'd bring the Sunday newspaper and read while we swam with dad.

He had to either borrow resident tickets from his brother, Johnny, who lived in Long Beach, or buy tickets, which he didn't care to do. If he didn't borrow them, he'd give the attendant a sob story, hoping they'd let us in, but it never worked. He often argued with them and threatened to take the attendant's name to "write a letter" of complaint. He'd also take the long way to avoid paying tolls, which in the long run, didn't pay.

Despite how it seemed, he wasn't a tightwad by any means. In fact, he was typically very generous. Just with certain things, he would be a penny pincher.

Once, dad saw a pretty girl at the beach and told us to call him "Uncle Carlo." My siblings thought it was funny, but it made me angry. Dad was vivacious and flirted with women all the time. Mom paid him no mind, but as young as I was, it bothered me.

At one point, I asked my mother to tell him she had a boyfriend that lived in the mailbox. She found it hilarious and silly but tried it anyway—it didn't work. He rolled his eyes at her.

One afternoon, my older brother was riding in the car with dad. They were stopped at a light. A girl walked by, and dad said, "What's cookin', good lookin'?"

He turned to dad and said, "That's not mom."

Dad meant no harm, and it never went beyond innocent flirting, but I wasn't a fan.

Darlene (far left) Carlo, baby Joseph, and Joann (far right)

My kids with dad

MOM

To describe my mother as a typical 50s housewife is on the right track. She married when she was nineteen and lived a sheltered life with her parents before that.

She dropped out of the traditional school system in the eighth grade and later headed to cosmetology school for a year before quitting that as well. She had a beautiful voice and was featured on a radio show from The Wally Jackson Studios. She babysat for relatives and adored being around her family and staying up late. Eventually, she got a job at a sewing factory where her aunts worked.

The job was to 'clean up' the threads sticking out on the clothes before the garments would go on to the next person. Once in a while, she'd accidentally cut a hole in a dress and bring it to her uncle.

"Giovanna, don't worry. You make a mistake; you bring to me. I fix for you," he'd offer in broken English.

She made her way over to her uncle many times.

One afternoon, a co-worker mentioned her nephew was stopping by because she told him about a beautiful girl she worked with—her. He was just out of the army and was excited to visit.

Dad was handsome and had a devilish smile that was hard to resist. Mom nearly fell off her chair when she saw him. She stood up to greet him but stumbled forwards. That was all it took to hook him.

They were married a year later.

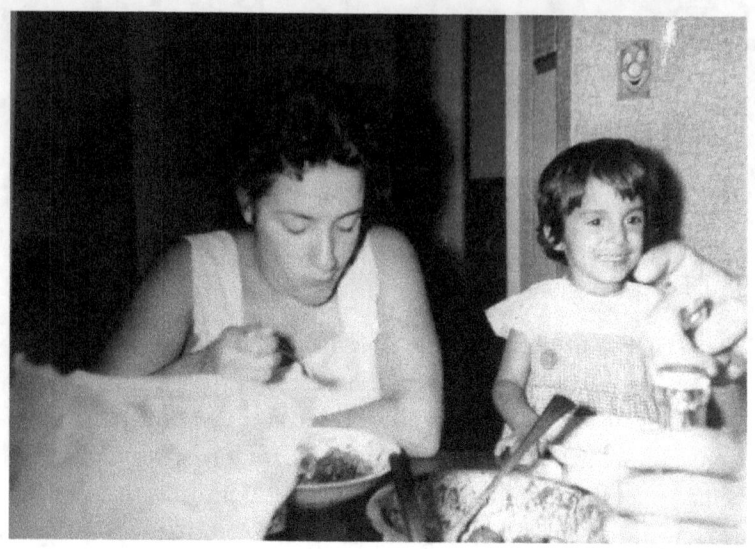

Me and mom

Mom was soft, quiet, and pretty, and Dad was hard, loud, and handsome. They were a perfect match, exact opposites to balance each other out. Together, they loved to sing and dance right in the middle of the living room. Once they started a family, however, routine settled in. It was roofing for dad and housecleaning, cooking, and taking care of babies for mom.

After settling in Corona, they rented out two other apartments. One to her mom and the other to Aunt Julia. We had many years of love and joy there. Holidays were so special, especially Christmas. We'd gather to share a grand meal, desserts, and gifts.

Christmas was the best time in my childhood. The preparations weeks in advance leading up to Christmas Eve was magical. Everyone would put up their trees and decorate. Aunt Julia would start baking, and once I got a whiff of the sweet, yeasty aroma of fresh dough, I couldn't get to her side fast enough. She made star cookies, gingerbread cookies, iced and sugar cookies with multi-colored sprinkles. She would make struffoli too, classic Italian honey balls made from dough, and dust a little powdered sugar on top.

Mouthwatering delights was what they were.

The gifts were nothing special, but anything wrapped can be exciting. We usually got clothes and shoes, things that were necessary instead of wanted. They were the best times.

Mom, grandma, and Aunt Julia shared in the cooking and took turns year after year, celebrating in each other's apartments.

Dad would talk about old times with grandpa, Uncle Jack, and Zio Antone as they played cards after the meal and gift giving was over. Raise a glass and toast to the future.

According to my dad, when mom got a visit from the "Red Bank," he planned to send her away for a few days, just to get a laugh from her—she was on her period. He used to ask my grandmother, his mother-in-law, if she, "Had the rag on." These terms used to fly right over my head. Grandma Laura was never offended by the term. She would laugh too. I think part of it was that he was so unapologetically himself, she just found him delightful.

Although amusing to some, when mom got her period, she did tend to turn into another person. PMS was not a term we heard of back then, but with her hormones raging and four kids underfoot, she'd go off the rails occasionally.

Once, when I was about twelve, my sister and I were playing outside, and she used the F word. I ran upstairs and told mom. I thought I was being clever. Maybe I'd get some brownie points for being good. But you know what they say about tattlers.

Mom called Joann upstairs and asked her if it was true. *Hmm,* I wondered if she would admit it.

"No."

Mom told her to go back outside, then walked me to my side of the bedroom and threw all of my things off the shelves with one swoop of her hand. Everything went flying. "Now clean it up." She slammed the door shut.

Well, that didn't go as planned.

I was non-verbally taught that any emotion, other than being happy, wasn't okay. I learned through being looked down on any time I was upset, angry, or sad. My mother was displeased with me, and although she wouldn't validate me, she also wouldn't take a moment to ask why I felt those feelings. I was instead told to, "Get over it," "Snap out of it," or to "Smile." And if I did offer an explanation, it was met with frustration and annoyance.

It was discouraging to open up, so I closed down.

Looking back, I don't think she had the wherewithal to deal with all the emotions or particularly knew what to say to offer comfort. I can only speak for myself, though. Every sibling has a different experience and perspective, even growing up in the same house with the same parents.

This was mine.

At night, my stomach would turn on its side, knowing bedtime was near. There were no rituals or bedtime stories. It was just, "Time for bed." Mom was exhausted and exasperated by then. She looked visibly wiped out. It must have been all she could do to get us in bed and have a little time to herself.

Mom pregnant with my brother Joe, my sister, Joann, brother Carlo, and me in front.

She was such a young wife and mother. Only twenty-four when I, her third child, was born. Mom was embarrassed to tell her own mother another was on the way.

Grandma would say, "Are you gonna be like your mother-in-law?" insinuating she would keep getting pregnant.

When she was thirty, mom had my brother, Joe, and she said she felt so old. Funny, because I had my first child at twenty-nine.

Years later, mom mentioned they never used protection. I teased her and asked if we were, "Oops one through four." She laughed and said she was surprised she didn't have many more.

Despite mom always being busy, I craved her attention. I adored her and wished for a small amount of time she might carve out just for me. If she was sitting on the sofa, I'd rest my head on her lap. For a few seconds, she'd touch my hair. I'd close my eyes and internally sigh. It felt heavenly, even if it lasted but a moment. I could have used a hug or mom asking me what I did in school that day or help with homework. But she kept four kids fed, clean, and safe, along with a husband that seemed to take up so much of her attention.

Once, I was sitting in my room playing on the floor, adjacent to the living room where mom and dad sat, and overheard dad say, "Don't you love Carlo just a little more than the others?"

I turned my ear closer to hear her answer.

"No," mom said. "I love them all the same."

I continued playing. I get it; they almost lost him when he was four years old to open heart surgery. He had a fifty percent chance to survive, which must have been brutal on them. He is and has been well since his surgery, thriving and has a family of his own.

My dad idolized him. They worked roofing together and grew a close bond over the years. Dad had a special place in his heart for Carlo.

She had a regular cleaning routine. Bathroom on Tuesdays, all floors on Thursdays, dusting on Mondays, with laundry on Wednesdays and Fridays. Dinner was on the table every night, and after cleaning up, it was baths and bed.

Joann, being five years my senior, was old enough to walk us to school. After she graduated, it was Carlo's turn until I could go by myself.

Mom didn't drive, so we walked everywhere. Food shopping must have been especially challenging for her, lugging the four of us and a wagon into town.

Once in a while, when she wasn't feeling overwhelmed, mom called for "Neck Time," which we were more than happy to oblige. We'd run to her and cuddled up for kisses.

THE BEASTLY STICK

My parents were raised differently.

Mom was brought up in a strict household, not allowed to go anywhere unaccompanied, not allowed to have friends over or play outside. She was sheltered and shielded from the world.

My dad was out and about the neighborhood, running with the tough guys. His father was in and out of their lives and had a heavy hand when disciplining. He told my siblings and me the short version of getting whipped and punched around, yet despite the abuse, he loved his dad dearly.

I asked why, and he shrugged and said, "He was my father. I loved him."

It was hard for me to understand how you could love someone who hurt you all the time. I don't think I could have if it had happened to me.

Having four kids of his own, he didn't continue that abuse onto us fortunately.

Mom had a stick beside the sofa, so if we go out of hand, she'd bang it on the couch and say, "You're gonna get it!" That was as far as 'hitting' got in our house though. All words and no action. We all felt safe enough with the knowledge that mom would never really use it.

Joann named the stick and had the audacity to write on it; "The Beastly Stick." Mom got a kick out of it, and that's how she referred to it from then on.

MY REFUGE

I was born in September 1959. The middle child, third in line of four, second girl. My sister, Joann, was extroverted and friendly, as well as our brother, Carlo. They both made friends easily. But I was unsure, felt inadequate, and was shy.

When I was by myself, I felt a sense of peace. There was always so much chatter in our house, it was hard to get quiet time. The noise around me, for the most part, was comforting, but there were moments when I longed to be alone.

There weren't any places to retreat to in all the chaos until we'd finally gotten our own rooms years later when Aunt Julia moved away. My parents didn't like the idea of renting to strangers, so they opened up the entire top floor and used both apartments. I got the front room, closest to my parents, because I was the scaredy cat in the family.

My bedroom had a closet that was deep and long, and I fit in it perfectly. There I would retreat when it got too loud or dad was shouting at someone. Or when it was storming. I was petrified of thunder, but inside the closet was my sanctuary. There was a light and an outlet. I brought a small record player inside and listened to music on my 45s. I tuned out the thunder and felt safe.

For many years before that, I shared a room with Joann. Double beds with a nightstand in between us. She was the neat one. Her side of the room was orderly, her clothes folded perfectly in her drawers. I, on the other hand, was not so inclined to keep a tidy room. My mother wouldn't tolerate an actual mess, though, so I kept in fairly clean, even if not to the same standards as my sister.

Listening to music and writing were my two outlets. Singing made me feel happy, sad, and every emotion in between. With writing, my imagination took flight. I could write anything I wanted to. I could make up stories and read them back to myself. I could save them and do rewrites. It was an escape from the hum-drum life I was leading.

There was nothing to look forward to. Just school, which I never enjoyed. Or summertime, which was always too far away or not filled with fun things to do.

In the summer, there were the days when the boys opened the fire hydrant—or as we called it, "the Johnny Pump." Kids would play outside, I'd walk to the park, albeit alone. When I was old enough to venture around on my own, I took long rides around the Lake. I even rode my bicycle to the World's Fair.

I had a few friends I spent some time with. Liliana lived a few houses from me. We'd sit in her driveway eating ice pops and reading Archie comic books. Sometimes, when I had a few dollars, I'd walk to Junction Boulevard to the record store and buy a 45, a smaller version of an album that had the main song on the A side and a second unknown song on the B side.

I liked to listen to the radio, especially on Saturday mornings—the top 100 with Casey Kasem.

The boys in the neighborhood began calling me "Tissue Girl." I paid them no mind, not knowing why, I did not put much thought into it, although I knew it was derogatory. After some time had passed, I found out why. They all assumed I was stuffing my bra, due to my tiny frame and not so tiny breasts. They weren't abnormally large, just large for me. They saw me getting out of dad's car after the beach one afternoon. I was still in my bathing suit when they realized there were no tissues to be found. Since then, the name calling ceased.

THE SEWING ROOM

I enjoyed spending time with Aunt Julia. She never had children of her own, though she had a nurturing side I adored. She was easygoing and laughed often. Her daily routine was to head down to her office in our basement and sew garments for clients. We had an extra room that was fairly large that was locked during off hours. She had two sewing machines, one for her and one for her brother, Zio Antone. They worked side by side from nine to five, only going upstairs for a lunch break.

My favorite thing to do was stand on a small stage that had a multi-hung mirror. It was there for her clients to step in front of and get fitted and sized for various dresses, but for me, it was to see multiples of myself pretending to be a Rockette.

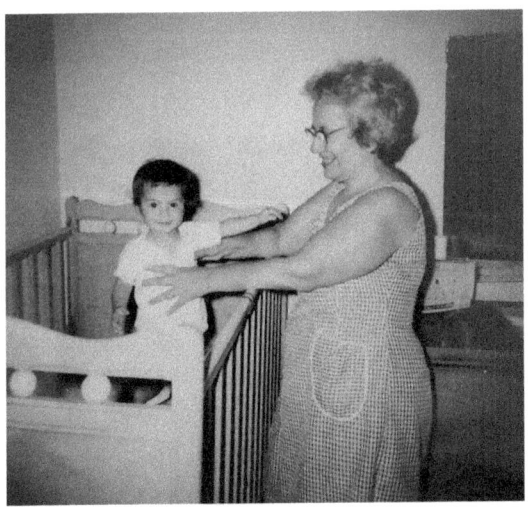

Me and Aunt Julia (DeeDoo)

Neither Zio nor Aunt Julia would scold me. I could touch the fabrics made of silk, satin, and chiffon. I could run my fingers through the colorful beads meant to be pinned into fake fruit or drape fabric over my tiny body to see how I would look if it were a dress. Aunt Julia's specialty was mostly formal wear for women: ball gowns, beaded evening dresses, wedding gowns, and fitted bodices with a tight waists and large flared skirts; one of which was my mother's wedding dress. It was exquisite, and I'd have loved to have worn it on my own wedding day, if only it hadn't been ruined in a flood.

Many of Aunt Julia's clients were wealthy, and some famous, but none that I can recall by name as they were never there when I visited. She would sometimes go to client's apartments in Manhattan when they couldn't travel to her. At times, I'd be asked to join her.

Those are some of my best memories.

ZIO ANTONE

Zio means Uncle in Italian. Antone was Anthony. To my siblings and I, he was known as Sindone, pronounced like the word condone. When we heard mom and grandma pronounce his name in Italian, we thought we heard, "Sindone," but no one seemed to notice, and we were never corrected.

He was born and raised in Vico Equense, Italy. I don't recall when Zio immigrated to America, as I was a small child, so I only have memories of him always being there. I do remember, however, that he had a wife and children he left behind. He called her once a month in the middle of the night because of the time difference. Never did she come to America to reunite or even visit. I found that odd but never thought to ask why.

He picked up some English after coming to America, but only a few words here and there. Maybe as many words as I picked up in Italian. He was 5'6" tall and thin for the most part, excluding his belly. It was large and accentuated by a belt. He wore a tucked in guinea tee, and open-toed backless sandals with white socks. He was mostly bald, but he had a patch of hair that lay like a horseshoe above his ears. Zio didn't have any teeth, which I found distractingly fascinating when he ate steak.

My siblings and I would run back and forth between Aunt Julia's apartment and Grandma Laura's, which was amusing to us, and only us. One evening, Uncle Zio wasn't having it. We were being noisy, and the more it annoyed Zio, the funnier we thought it was. Normally, we weren't bratty kids, but there were days that were the exception.

Uncle Jack sat stoic in his wing-backed chair, chugging a gallon of red wine straight from the bottle. Aunt Julia giggled at us and turned her attention back to the TV. Zio's chair was identical to Uncle Jack's. They were flanking the living room entrance, making it easy for us to stand behind him and pat him on the head.

Zio mumbled something in Italian. We giggled more. But eventually, even with a pretty good amount of patience, Zio couldn't take it anymore. He shot to his feet, his arms flailing, and shouted, "Tutti fuori!" meaning, "all out!"

Although we didn't understand him, somehow, we did as we were told and ran back to our apartment.

Sindone and me

40

CANDY CIGARETTES

"Vai al negozio per me," Zio Antone barked as he waved a dollar bill at Joann.

She tilted her head in confusion.

In our house, they used the second language as a way to talk without us understanding. Though it would have been better, perhaps, to teach us Italian and just talk about certain things when we weren't around.

"Kent-a Cigaret," He waved her away. "Vai, ora!"

She grabbed the dollar and went to Jacks. When she returned, he was livid. And when an Italian is livid, that can be scary, especially when you don't understand them.

"Che diavolo e' questo? Kent-a cigarette, capisci?" he urged.

Her eyes widened. Of course, she thought. After all, why would he want candy cigarettes? "Okay, got it!"

He smiled, though still scolded her a little. "No candito cigarette."

Off she went to buy the real thing, bringing him back his Kents and his change.

INCOMING

As I said earlier, my father worked a full-time job as a roofer, except when there was inclement weather. Sometimes, he seemed to be home more than he was at work. With occasional time on his hands, he took on remodeling our one and only bathroom. It didn't solve the six people to one bath ratio, but it was nice when it was finished.

Just as he demolished the floor and tiled walls, he was called back to work—leaving a gaping hole in the floor. Walking to the toilet was a formidable challenge. I don't remember why dad took it down to the joists, but it unfortunately opened up Rose's bathroom ceiling. Dad had no other choice but to show us, one by one, how to step carefully and slowly on each floor beam to make it to the potty and to explain to Rose that he'd fix it as soon as he could.

She came up with a novel idea to shield herself from spying eyes by sitting with an umbrella.

Dad got his orders to finish the job before something embarrassing happened, but it was too late.

Call it bad timing or an inopportune moment, but Carlo and Rose had to go at the same time. Her umbrella wasn't opened yet, and Carlo didn't follow the slow and steady rule. Losing his balance, he fell through the floor and grabbed onto one of the boards. His legs dangled in front of Rose.

Screaming ensued, and all of her dignity was lost. Needless to say, dad finished the floor that weekend.

He tried to keep busy on his time off, and one afternoon, he decided to work on his car in the backyard. The hood was up, and his face was buried in the nuts and bolts and grease of the mechanics. It was a summer's day and all his car windows were open while he worked. He heard a high-pitched noise and peeked his head up over the hood to investigate. Nothing seemed unusual though, so he returned to his car until he heard it again. But this time, he noticed something moving inside the car in the back seat.

Upon a closer look, he spotted a Capuchin monkey!

Although he was initially surprised, dad thought it was adorable and smiled. The monkey almost seemed to smile back. Just as he wondered what he should do next, however, the cute little monkey began throwing all of his papers in the air that he had so neatly organized the day before.

Dads smile turned into an angry stare, and the monkey seemed to pick up on his mood change. The animal's expression changed too and it squeaked a high-pitch scream before tearing ass down the block. Dad ran after the little fella, but he was too fast.

When he told us about his adventure, we wished we'd been there to see it.

It seems a neighbor owned the Capuchin monkey, and it got loose, but they were reunited a while later.

JOHNNY PUMP

Summer was a time for us to have fun and play outside until the streetlights turned on.

The boys played Scully with bottle caps in the street, where they would shoot their chips (bottle caps), trying to land each chip onto a box and get it farther than the other player, going from box one to thirteen and back to one again.

The girls jumped rope and played hopscotch, where they would use chalk to draw squares with numbers in them and throw a stick or rock into a square. Hopping over to it, they'd grab the object and hop back to the beginning, without messing up your steps.

There was also handball and stoopball and much bicycle riding.

When the temperature was unbearable, the boys would turn on the Johnny Pump, which got its name from the New York Fire Brigade after its inventor, John Giraud. There would be a whirl of excitement as everyone ran inside to change clothes.

Mothers sat on the front steps and watched with enthusiasm. Kids took turns going under the stream while a neighborhood boy named Louie held a can over the flow to ease the sting and intensity of the water. When everyone was eventually cooled off, playing would resume. Some would change into dry clothes while others opted to air dry.

The jingle from Mr. Softy would send everyone scattering to their houses again to fetch some change to buy ice cream. Sometimes we got a yes, other times it was a no.

The days were long, and we tried to hold onto every second we didn't have to go back to school.

HANDS OFF THE WALLS

My Grandmother Laura and my mom spent a fair amount of their mornings deep in their cleaning routine. I can vividly remember grandma with a bottle of furniture polish in one hand, a lemon oil rag in the other. The chemically sterile scent of blench mixed with a sharp citrus hung heavy in the air.

When we dashed in and out of grandma's apartment, we'd often touch the walls, leaving fingerprints and smudges everywhere.

"Hands off the walls!" she'd say as she chased behind us with a soapy rag.

Grandma Laura and Grandpa Angelo (Maternal grandparents)

They cooked dinner every night in their own apartments, but we'd all eat together on Sundays at Grandma Laura's. Meatballs and macaroni, with a bottle of red wine and a loaf of Italian bread. Although this meal was served promptly at one o'clock in the afternoon, it was considered dinner, and nothing would be served in the evening.

If you showed up after the sauce was placed, grandma would say, "The plate doesn't wait for you. You wait for the plate!"

Grandpa would fire up the record player with Connie Francis, Vic Damone, or Frank Sinatra. Our uncle would play Elvis when he could.

Us kids were the first ones to leave the table, ready to resume outdoor play. The adults would linger and eat fruit or crack open roasted nuts.

PAPER PEOPLE

Mrs. Biederman, my fourth grade history teacher, assigned the class weekend homework—dioramas, something I'd never heard of before. We had those two days to buy or collect supplies and come in Monday morning with a finished piece, along with an information sheet.

It was explained to us that a diorama was a model that showed a scene with three-dimensional figures, large or small, standing in front of a painted background.

To my horror, I didn't have supplies to make a diorama, but I managed to find a shoe box and turned it on its side. I drew a picture of a blue sky with clouds and taped it to the background. I had green construction paper and laid it out as grass. My biggest challenge was the people. I drew them on looseleaf, which was a bad idea, and taped them in a standing position. Not 3D, but that was the best I could do with what I had available. I wasn't proud of it and wondered if I should even bother bringing it in or if I should instead make an excuse as to why I didn't.

In the end, there I was on Monday morning carrying it to school. The slightest little breeze kept compromising my paper people. In a way, it was funny walking to school with a shoe box and some scotch tape holding it all together.

Everyone placed their dioramas on the table at the back of the classroom. You could pick mine out from a mile away. Pathetic, I thought. I scanned the others, impressed by their creativity. Some used action figures, others used mini dolls. I especially liked the ones that used real tree branches, rocks, moss, and soil as part of the background.

The ones made from nature, well, I certainly could have done the same if I'd only thought of it.

When our grades were given the next day, I was pleasantly surprised by a C. Mrs. Biederman probably gave me points for doing it without help.

DEEDOO

A special treat with my favorite person, Aunt Julia. Ice cream. Chocolate, vanilla, and strawberry.

After a bath, I was all powered up and ready for TV. Aunt Julia—aka DeeDoo, as Joseph, my baby brother, dubbed her after finding it difficult to say her name—would ask me to fetch her and myself a bowl just before we'd settle down and watch a show. I noticed ice crystals forming but kept scooping. I sat with her as we dug in. It tasted different, but I had no idea it was stale. I knew it was off in some way, but it was never an issue because the best part of eating that ice cream was being with her.

"Sleep over tonight!" Joseph said excitedly. Zio was in Italy for the month, and it was Friday night, so mom was letting us sleep over at Aunt Julia's. Joe and I opened the sofa bed and pushed another fold-out mattress over to accommodate the three of us. Joe and I both wanted the coveted spot of sleeping next to Aunt Julia, so she was in the middle of the two mattresses.

After a movie, we fell sleep although Aunt Julia's snoring eventually woke me up. As I readjusted myself, I noticed a space between my mattress and the one Aunt Julia and Joe were on. The louder she snored, the more the mattress shifted away.

I leaned over her and shook Joe. "She's gonna fall," I whispered, pointing to the space between Aunt Julia and me. "The mattress is moving."

He jumped off the bed and ran over to my side. I got out of bed too, and we tried to push it together again. We did the best we could, then crawled back into the sheets and went back to sleep.

Shortly after I'd drifted off again, there was a loud boom.

Joe and I looked up—Aunt Julia was on the floor!

We froze, then checked if she was hurt, but what we saw set us off. She was laughing so hard, she was turning red.

As we calmed down, we helped her up, and I gave up my spot so she wouldn't fall again. It was times like those that endeared my heart to hers.

THE NUMBER SEVEN

The IRT Number Seven train was a hop, skip, and jump from our house, just down the block and over one street to Roosevelt Avenue.

The elevated train took Aunt Julia and me to Manhattan for a visit with one of her clients. The ride was a short thirty minutes, but to me, it seemed to take forever.

As always, Aunt Julia took her newspaper along and thumbed through it. I was prepared this time with my own reading material. I whipped out my Communion Bible and proceeded to look busy, when I noted a man sitting opposite us smiling at me. It was more of a gentle laugh that he tried to suppress. I shifted in my seat and dropped my eyes back to my book.

When I looked up and again, the man was still smiling from ear to ear. His shoulders shook and his eyes twinkled. He reminded me of Louis Armstrong. I moved closer to Aunt Julia. She looked down at me, then glanced at the man and laughed too.

She reached for my book and turned it right side up. My face flushed hot, and I lost myself in her armpit.

Manhattan was alive, more so than Queens or anywhere else I'd ever been. Which was mainly just Queens and occasionally the Bronx or Brooklyn. It had an energy about it that was easy to get caught up in. It felt exciting and full of promise.

Aunt Julia held my hand as we crossed 5th Avenue. We bumped shoulders with people rushing around us, the aroma of roasting chestnuts filling our nostrils. Flyers were shoved in faceless faces. Aunt Julia squeezed my hand and veered me away. Our steps were purposeful and quick, like everyone else around us.

"Here we are," Aunt Julia said as she turned into a posh apartment building on Park Avenue. A man in a blue suit with gold trim and white gloves held the door for us. Aunt Julia nodded and mouthed, "Thank you.'"

The lobby was decorated for Christmas, and I'd never seen a tree so grand. My mouth dropped open, and Aunt Julia smiled at the awe I was in. Magical, just magical.

We walked to the elevator, and she let me push the up button. Ding, the bell rang, and doors split open. Another man in a blue suit with gold trim stood tall and regal inside the elevator with us and said in a stately manner, "Lobby."

He held the button as we stepped inside. A gilded mirror sat hugely proud on the wall. I could see the Christmas tree adornments sparkled behind us before the doors closed and whisked us away. The man hit the Penthouse button, and my stomach jumped as we ascended. The doors to the little box that brought us to the Penthouse opened again, and what greeted us wasn't what I expected.

"Ladies," he said. He swayed his arm outwardly, ushering us forward and through the doors.

We were somehow already in her client's apartment. There were no corridors to walk down, no other apartments to shuffle past.

"Good morning, Julia! Who do we have here?" A pretty housekeeper with a warm smile beamed down at me.

"My niece, Darlene," Aunt Julia introduced us. "This is Pansy."

I smiled shyly as she took our coats and bags. "Make yourself at home, Darlene. Take a look around, and I'll have lunch for you at noon."

I followed Aunt Julia, who seemed to know where she was going.

We passed many an elegant room I was sure to revisit later. As Aunt Juila unpacked her supplies, she got right to work and I told her I was going to have a look around.

Pansy stopped by with a teapot and two cups. "Make sure you go see the library," she said with a smile. Excited at all this beauty surrounding me, I nodded and headed back where we started from.

I peeked into the kitchen. Pansy was back already too, humming and smiling as she worked. I went unnoticed.

The dining room was a huge area with the usual furniture, a table and chairs, a China cabinet and server. But it was all so exquisite, the only word I could use to possibly describe it. Cream-colored fabrics on the windows and chairbacks with matching damask silk. There was a large floral centerpiece with fresh pink roses that reminded me of spring, even though it was mid-December.

The table was set for a service of eight. There were gold-trimmed dinner plates, antique Baroque flatware, cloth napkins, and a bucket just waiting for ice and a champagne bottle. It was all impressive, particularly at my age. Something special to behold. I also spied a crystal bowl behind the doors of the China cabinet filled with chocolates.

Just one, I thought, but I didn't dare open the doors and take one without asking permission. Even still, my mouth watered. *No*, I swallowed and kept walking.

I finally found the library, and it was no wonder Pansy suggested it. It was spectacular—so bright it made me squint. No curtains on the floor-to-ceiling windows. They beckoned me over. The dark hardwoods creaked as I stepped forward and closed my eyes, letting the sun warm my face. It made me a bit sleepy, though, and I thought briefly of taking a nap.

With how high up we were, the people down below were tiny dots. The streets were littered with traffic: taxis, buses, and cars, all driving without abandon. It was a miracle there weren't more accidents the way they sideswiped one other and had no time for regulations. I pressed my face against the windowpane, only to quickly pulled away from the heat of the glass.

There was so much to explore in that room alone.

The clink of Pansy stacking dishes while humming echoed into the library, and the smell of lemon furniture polish wafted through the air. There were so many pleasant scents, it was hard not to smile. I whirled around and got dizzy before finding a chair to gain my balance.

As tall as the windows were, the bookshelves were even higher. They were built-ins, some stacked straight while others leaned crooked. The two sets of wing-backed chairs that flanked the bookshelves served as a place to sit with a book and get lost in a world you may have otherwise never known.

I slipped off my shoes and rubbed my socked feet over the plush ruby rug beneath me. I flipped the gold fringe up with the tips of my toes, then smoothed it down. I must have spent quite a bit of time in there, as I was soon called to lunch.

I met Aunt Julia back where I left her. She placed her needles and sewing kit aside as Pansy wheeled our lunch into the room on a fancy gold and glass cart. We had finger sandwiches with the crust cut off. They were stacked this way and that on a serving tray with sliced carrots and celery on the side. A large pitcher of lemonade was poured into fancy glasses, and a napkin was placed on each of our laps before Pansy left us, closing the door behind her.

As we dug in, I looked at all the accessories around me. Assorted threads of many colors, buttons, and sequins. Satin fabric in the shade of warm cocoa lay over a chair. The lace was of the same color. It was halfway sewn on, and there was still more work to do.

I reached over and touched the Tulle that peeked out from the hem. It felt like sandpaper under my fingers but looked so elegant. I put my sandwich down and went to sit on a moss-colored velvet-tufted otto-man with gold fringe at the bottom. Aunt Julia hadn't moved from the brown damask chair.

It took her a little longer to finish her meal, but eventually she took a long drink of lemonade. "Back to work," she said with a giggle. She showed me a picture of the finished dress, and what it would look like when done.

"Can I see it before we go?" I asked.

Her eyes twinkled and her cheeks grew rosy. She gently quivered as she giggled. Her voice was pitched high as she tried to speak through the laughter. "I won't finish this today! It's gonna take me another month, at least."

I shrugged and went off to find that China cabinet again. This time, I quietly opened the doors and took a chocolate, popping it in my mouth, my hesitation gone. Most delicious. I went back for another, feeling less guilty the second time.

Aunt Julia worked until five o'clock, then we made our way to the train station.

Manhattan was alive even more so at Christmastime. Santa was on every corner, ringing his bell. Colored lights twinkled from store fronts and trees. Smoke emanated from manhole covers and car horns honked intermittently. Hot dog stands were a staple in New York, and when you smelled one, you'd gulp and yearn for them.

Catching the Number Seven and getting two seats together in rush hour was a small miracle I appreciated. I leaned on Aunt Julia's shoulder, closed my eyes, and fell asleep.

JACKS

Down the block and around a multi-story apartment building was the IRT (Interborough Rapid Transit) Number Seven train that ran from Flushing, Queens to Times Square, Manhattan. As funny as it sounds, that train system kept me from feeling alone. As I lay awake at night, struggling to fall asleep, the clickety-clack and whistling soothed me to sleep. The squeal of the breaks and the ding of the bell as the doors opened and closed were welcome.

Someone, somewhere, was awake too, a signal that helped me feel safe enough to fall asleep. Although it took too long for another train to come again, it also left quickly.

Under the El (elevated train) was Jack's corner candy store. It should have had a revolving door because all the kids on 39th Avenue and beyond were in and out of there daily. It was a small, narrow store, dimly lit with old wooden floorboards that squeaked and moved under our feet. The counter took up almost the entire length of the store, except for the telephone booths in the rear. It had silver stools with red cushions that were much too high for me.

When you walked in, there was a small cubby with a register behind it and shelves with several varieties of candy in the front: wax lips, Tootsie Rolls, fruit striped gum, candy buttons on paper tape, candy cigarettes, Mary Janes, and bubble gum. Oh, how I loved candy! They had tons of chips and a soda fountain, too. There were also pretzel jars every few inches apart all along the counter with long salted stick pretzels.

Pepe was a stranger to me, really. Not a relative or friend, just a man dressed in a tweed jacket and tie. Slicked back dark hair, balding, beady eyes, and a mustache that was heavily waxed and turned up at the ends. The creepiest looking man I'd ever seen. Maybe it was the mustache. He was a regular at Jack's. He just stood there by the newspapers and candy bars, one arm up, leaning on a shelf, Jack by the register. He occasionally lifted his hand to his mouth and puffed on an oversized cigar, sending clouds of stinky smoke into my lungs. The pungent haze circled around his face, and it made me lose my breath.

Bumping into him was not ideal as I tried to just buy bubble gum and leave.

My dad happened to be there once, talking and laughing with both Pepe and Jack.

"Come here and give Pepe a kiss, it's his birthday!" my dad said. Just the thought of it made me cower. I shook my head no and scrunched up my face.

"Come on, one little kiss?" Pepe said, bending down and puckering up.

I ran behind the register to get away from him. I stood behind Jack and the three men laughed. When I felt I could, I darted out of the store as fast as I could, happy to have escaped that one!

SWEET DREAMS, YOU PAIN IN THE ASS

Bedtime was stressful for me. Although I reveled in silence, I never liked the quiet or the dark at bedtime. At night, falling asleep before everyone else was the best thing I could do, but that almost never happened.

There I would lay, listening for Zio Antone, hoping he would make a call to Italy late at night. The bedroom I shared with Joann had another door that was sealed but led to Aunt Julia's apartment. We could hear him talking, and when he did, his voice was boisterous, lively, and energetic. The house dark and still, with everyone else was asleep, I found his calls comforting in the absence of train rumblings.

Most nights, I hoped dad was still awake in the living room or that Rose was watching TV downstairs. She wore a hearing aid and turned the volume all the way up. The noise helped me feel safe and made it easier to fall asleep.

At times, as dad watched TV, I'd ask if I could lie on the couch until I fell asleep beside him. He'd usually say yes, if I lay still. He laughed at how literal I took that. "I didn't mean you should sleep like a soldier!"

"No!" Joann would say when mom asked her to hold my hand until I could fall asleep.

"Yes," said my mother. Along with that, my mom kept the light on over the kitchen sink just for me. The kitchen was next to our room.

Joann did not appreciate that. "You stupid little shit. You're a scaredy cat. What a baby."

She once traced her finger on the icy window that was an arm's-length from her bed. "I love Pat," she wrote. The glass made a squeaking sound with each swipe. Mom came rushing in. She thought I was crying until Joann told her it was her making the noise. It was times such as those that strangely enough also helped me fall asleep. Her insults could have just as well been lullabies.

GRANDPA ANGELO

Grandpa Angelo, my maternal grandfather, was short in stature and bald, just like Zio Antone. He was born in Tampa, Florida, then moved to New York in his teens. He wore many hats in his life. He was once a professional boxer nicknamed, "The Greenpoint Thunderbolt" because he lived in Greenpoint, Brooklyn. He later owned a barbershop and worked for the City of New York in the Purchasing Department. He kept that job until he retired at sixty-five.

He had a pension and good medical insurance, he used to proudly boast. He made sure he and Laura would be set after retirement and not have to worry about paying medical bills.

I remember him coming home every night and changing clothes behind his closet door. He'd wash up for dinner, then spend the rest of the night watching shows in his apartment with grandma.

He married Laura in 1932 during the Great Depression. They lived modestly, not doing anything remotely extravagant. Eating out at restaurants was very rare, usually only if they attended a party. Grandma usually made low-budget meals, such as pasta fagioli, which consists of any short pasta, beans, and tomato sauce, minestrone soup, and on Sundays—which became a tradition for our family—was spaghetti and meatballs. And although on a budget, her food was always delicious.

As the family grew, the table seemed smaller during our gatherings in their apartment. Even though we squeezed in, there were memories you can't beat.

Whenever I'd waltz into grandma and grandpa's apartment, my grandfather would shout, "Picciridda," which means "little girl" in a Sicilian dialect.

Grandma gave me a comeback in which I happily used. "Mi scipparu a cullana!" which means, "Leave me alone."

The way I heard it, he seemed to shout to me, "Bitchadeeda," and I would say, "New-Ma-Sa-Ca." No wonder he'd laugh like a belly full of jelly!

He loved ice cream, so much so that for his birthday one time, mom thought it would be funny if we put a half gallon of vanilla, chocolate, and strawberry on a plate and hand it to him. Well, he ate the entire half gallon!

My maternal grandfather, Angelo with his vegetable garden

Grandpa could be stubborn when he got angry and hold a grudge, but he could also be persuaded to make up if we tried hard enough.

He had a tiny hole just above his lip, and we kids asked him about it once. He said it was his bank, that he kept his money there so it would be safe. Hmm, good one—a chicken pox scar, for sure.

THE HYENA IS A BULLY

Catholic school was a place I spent eight years of my life. Everything about it made me nervous. The nuns were uptight and strict, always ready to crack someone on the hand with a metal ruler for any number of reasons, or for nothing at all. I was in a constant state of anxiety. Luckily, I was never scolded by my teachers. I kept to myself because I was shy and insecure. I had little confidence to speak up or ask questions for fear I would be laughed at.

I had one true friend named Yvonne, who moved away after the third grade. I grew up with my classmates, the same faces every day for eight years, although I had a rude awakening while in my last grade of school.

Word had gotten around that a few girls were coming after me. One classmate was telling everyone she was going to pulverize me. I was oblivious to having enemies, especially Lorraine, Amelia, and another girl whose name escapes me. We weren't the best of friends, but I found them fun to be around, especially Amelia.

Mrs. Marcasie was our music teacher and would get especially frustrated with Amelia and her antics. So much so, she called her the "Laughing Hyena." Mrs. Marcasie didn't give her that moniker because she found her delightful. She called her that because Amelia couldn't stop laughing during class. Mrs. Marcasie would tremble and bite her bottom lip. She would scream at her, spitting while she told her to "Shut up," shaking her crooked and arthritic fingers at her. But that only made Amelia laugh louder.

Rumors were gaining momentum that Amelia wanted to beat me up and leave a scar on my face. I worried constantly, and my apprehension grew.

On the day she decided she would finally come after me, I felt the tension. Amelia was especially cocky in class that afternoon. She'd given me the side-eye and turned to her fellow cohorts, smiling devilishly. I had all the normal feelings one gets when they know they'll be pounded into the earth. My palms were sweaty, my heart raced, and the lump in my throat felt like a boulder—I was petrified.

The bell jolted me out of my seat, and I gathered my books, perhaps a little slower than usual. I clutched them to my chest, as if to shield myself as I began my walk home, the same route I took for eight years.

I didn't see them until I heard that old, familiar laugh. Then their footsteps grew louder and more frantic. After we were a reasonable distance from the school, she lunged at me. I braced myself as she dug her fingers deep into my scalp and pulled me backward. Amelia lifted me off the sidewalk and dropped me onto my back. It's difficult to defend yourself when you're attacked from behind, but clearly, I was already no match for her. Even if I had been facing her, she was twice my size in every direction, and I was the tiniest student ever to be measured for a uniform in our school.

My books were scattered about and a crowd had gathered. No one asked her to stop or came to see if I was okay. Her chubby fingers were still embedded in my hair. When she pulled her hand away, a good amount of strands went with her. She stepped on my face and reached down to run her fingernail across the side of my left eye. There was a musty smell from the bottom of her dirty shoe, but it mattered little compared to the sting from her fingernail when she ripped open the skin above my eye.

Blood leaked from not only my eye but my nose as well. Her foot had covered my entire face.

The crowd thinned as she stepped over me. Trembling, I pushed through the pain and gathered my books. Both of my knees were bleeding too. It must have happened when I turned over, trying to get up.

I didn't cry, but tears welled.

I never found out why she disliked me so much, when all along I thought we friends. And I never told anyone.

Tucked into the safety of my room, I retreated to my closet and sat there until dinner was ready. I'd always felt invisible, but never more than that day.

THE ROADRUNNER

Uncle Jack was four feet tall. He had a small head and a huge belly. He wore his pants up over his tummy with a belt tightly wrapped around his ample waist. He had beady eyes and a bulbous nose. The funniest thing I remember about him was his nickname, "The Roadrunner." It was funny because it was the opposite of everything he was.

The Roadrunner was quick and ran around from place to place, was tall and thin, not anything like Uncle Jack.

Joann's boyfriend gave him that name.

Joann, Uncle Jack (AKA The Roadrunner), and Carlo

To see him walk around was fascinating. He shuffled his feet when he walked, which made it look as though he should be moving at a swift pace, only he hardly made a stride, so it took him a great deal of time to get from here to there.

To me, he was an old man married to DeeDoo who sat in a chair nursing a bottle of vino. Unlike Zio, he spoke good English, but rarely spoke. I had no feelings for him one way or the other. He hardly interacted with anyone in the family and spoke so few words, it was almost as though he was in a trance-like state. He was odd, perhaps inebriated. He walked around unhurriedly and seemed to have no responsibility whatsoever.

As far back as I can remember, he didn't work. I heard he was a doorman back in the day, though. It was his wife, Aunt Julia, and his brother-in-law, Zio Antone, who took to the sewing room daily to earn a living. His only activity, besides drinking, was going to the market occasionally. He'd wheel his cart behind him and travel at a snail's pace into town. He'd return with a bag or two a few hours later.

One item he always pulled out of a brown bag was a gallon of wine. He made sure he had one opened and one closed, just so he wouldn't run out.

I saw little interaction between him and Aunt Julia. They seemed to talk only when necessary, and even then, just a few words here and there. They didn't have a good marriage because of the way he treated her when they were younger—I'd heard stories of him being physically abusive.

One of the kindest souls I have ever known was my aunt. To imagine her being treated in such a way makes me sad.

I think he was fortunate that she let him live with her. Let him sit there day after day and nurse his wine. He had no redeeming qualities, and from the goodness of her heart, she allowed him to stay.

One day, he went into the hospital and never came home. When he passed away, it was all so very unemotional. Not only for me, but for all of us.

PATIENCE OF A SAINT

When I was in first grade, Sister St. Raymond was my teacher. She was also a nun, and she left a lasting impression on me for her kindness and patience. There was a lot of patience to be had when it came to me learning math.

To say it took a ton of nerve for me to tell her that I didn't understand the assignment was an understatement. But there I was, three feet nothing, sauntering up to her desk, paper and pencil in hand. She explained the math to me without a fuss though, and then sent me on my way.

It didn't take long before I was back in front of her again, however, shaking my head when she asked if I understood.

After the third time, I saw a twinkle in her eyes and she grinned. She patted her lap for me to jump aboard. Arm around me, she held my pencil in her hand and repeated the rules of mathematics, hoping this time it would stick.

Nothing.

She looked down at me and nodded to see if I understood, but I shook my head. She sent me back to my desk, telling me it was okay. At that point, I was just not getting it and she didn't want to overwhelm me. After that she spent a little extra time with me, teaching me with great patience. I learned mathematics and was promoted to the next grade.

MRS. JANKOWSKI

When I was in second grade, we had our annual play to prepare for. Each grade would put on a show, and our theme was a combination of scenes from various movies set to music. I was in a wedding scene, but I don't recall what movie it was from.

I played the bride, and Thomas Jankowski played the groom. We were the main attraction at the closing act.

I was lucky and honored that Aunt Julia made the gown I was to wear. She didn't mince product or design. She used lace, satin, and beautiful while pearls.

Me as a bride in a school play. Aunt Julia made me that gown.

Our entrance song was, "Somewhere, My Love." Mrs. Marcasie played the piano.

We were waiting in the wings for our turn when Thomas peed on himself. Poor fellow, he looked so embarrassed and uncomfortable. With only myself and the teacher aware, he was rushed away but soon returned to stand next to me. Luckily, they had an extra pair of slacks for him to change into.

Mrs. Marcasie, fraught with her usual anxiety, pounded the piano keys, and we stepped forward onto the stage. Our play was a success.

THE FAINTING GAME

"Breathe in," my sister commanded. "Count to twenty, now breathe out." Her victims, I mean friends, did as she said while she ever so lightly squeezed her fingers around their necks. It was a game, she told them. She could make them pass out.

It was astonishing how many volunteers she had. One by one, they lined up to see if it would work.

Nothing. No one had passed out. All day long, and not one person had dropped.

After dinner and a bath, we sat around the living room and told mom about the fainting game. I told Joann to try it out on me, and she was all too eager to do so. Mom didn't object, most likely because she paid little attention to it being dangerous.

Joann wrapped her fingers around my neck and told me to count. The first thing I remember afterward was a terrific slap across the face by Carlo, who then carried me into the kitchen upon Mom's command.

"If your father sees this, he is going to hit the roof!" She seemed more worried about dad yelling than anything else.

I was disoriented and blurted, "It works!"

DROWNING

I was nine in 1968. Nothing much was going on that summer, except for playing outside and trips to the beach on Sundays although one afternoon, my sister took me to a pool party.

She was fourteen, and her boyfriend, Pat, was going to be there. He lived across the street from us. They'd been together since they were ten. As a quiet kid, I was shy around him and all of her friends, but I still went to the party regardless, even though I couldn't swim.

Most of her friends were swimming and throwing a ball around. Pat ran past me, then looped around and stopped behind me. As I turned to see what he was doing, his cool, wet arms grabbed me around my waist. He hoisted me into the air and threw me into the pool.

I sunk like a concrete brick. I tried to get back to the top as I gasped for air. I heard muffled laughing above the water.

When my head momentarily popped up through the surface, I choked and coughed. Then down I sunk again, and at that point, I knew I was on my own. I had to save myself. Finally, after trying to get my head above water once more, I made my way to the edge, grabbed on and hauled myself out.

I couldn't breathe and coughed up water from my mouth and nose.

As soon as I could, I went inside the house, grabbed my clothes, and ran home.

That was the first drowning experience, and I should have learned how to swim after that—but I didn't. There weren't many opportunities to do so, and the ocean isn't a safe place to try.

I was told I would be going to summer camp. Mom sent me for two weeks to a non-sleep away program. I was picked up each morning and dropped off every night in front of my house by a school bus. It wasn't something I enjoyed or wanted to do. I don't recall being asked if I even wanted to, but I also don't remember ever telling my mom I'd rather be home.

I felt inadequate around groups of kids, especially strangers. I had no clue how to make friends and felt uncomfortable doing the activities they asked of us.

One of them was swimming.

I was told to change into a bathing suit and go into the pool area. As I stood, watching everyone having fun, diving in and running around, a hand passed against my back, and I was shoved into the water.

This time, it wasn't a six-foot pool—it was a ten-foot, and just like before, I went straight to the bottom.

It was a long way down.

When I reached the bottom, I pushed on the padded floor with all of my might but came up short. I sunk down again, then gave it everything I had. I pushed my feet as hard as I could and reached for the edge. I grabbed the slippery floor and lifted myself out.

I ran over to a counselor and told her what happened, but all she said was that I should get right back into the water and learn how to swim.

With no one to help me, I found a seat a safe distance away.

My two weeks at camp was about done, and I couldn't be happier. When I got home, mom said Aunt Julia paid for another two weeks of camp for me. So, I was quietly shipped off to another camp for an additional two long weeks. This time though, with no incidents.

I was happy when it was over.

THE SEANCE

The early 70s was not necessarily a time of paranormal investigations and having your fortune read, nonetheless, my sister, brother, and her friends decided to hold a seance in the basement.

Our basement was not a place I enjoyed being alone. The boiler room scared me, and I would always speedwalk past it to get to Aunt Julia's sewing room. I'd play down there when my sister and her friends were there too, but avoided going alone. If I did ever venture down, I'd always run back up the steps, leaving the lights on, which I would later get yelled at for.

That day, I was invited to join them, but immediately declined. I had no intentions of being scared to death. However, I didn't want to miss a chance to see if any of our dearly departed would make an appearance or if the others would be scared to death.

I had an idea that would help them along a little. I wasn't sure if it would work, but the thought delighted me.

I went to get a toy we had upstairs and ran back down as fast as I could. We had a Laugh Box. It was a square box that fit in my hand with a clown face on it. His red nose was a button, and when you pushed it, it would laugh.

The others prepared themselves around a small table with chairs. They turned off the lights, closed their eyes, and invoked the spirits. My brother asked loudly for a sign, and they waited.

Nothing happened. I wanted to build up suspense before I hit the clown nose.

Several more times, they asked for a sign, then one of the girls said, "Who is here with us? Can you make a noise?"

That's when I pressed the nose.

Unfamiliar laughter filled the quiet basement. It took a second for them to respond. Then, at once, every chair was shoved out from under them and they screamed. Footsteps hurled toward the staircase.

"Run!" they shouted.

I laughed quietly—until I realized there was no time to get out of there and slipped behind the open door. A wind kicked up as they ran past.

I never told them the truth. The story lives on to this very day.

HIDE AND GO SUFFOCATE

There was nothing like a game of Hide and Go Seek when it was raining and there was nothing else to do.

"Come with me," Joann whispered in my ear. "Carlo is gonna count, and we're gonna hide. Whoever he doesn't find, wins."

We were in the basement, so I thought I'd slip into Grandpa Angelo's storage area. It was a square cut out underneath the staircase.

"No, I have a better spot," Joann said, grabbing my arm and pulling me toward the refrigerator instead. She opened the door and told me he'd never find me in there.

I stepped in and she pushed the door closed. A few minutes passed, and the door swung open. Dad grabbed me forcefully, pulling me toward him. He was yelling at Joann, telling her I could have suffocated.

She merely said, "Sorry," and went on her merry way.

MISSION SUNDAY

F eeling anxious at every turn for no apparent reason summed up my nine years at OLS (Our Lady of Sorrows). If there was a knock on the door while class was in session, surely it was me they were coming for. If they whispered in the teacher's ear to discuss why they had come, I was certain it was because of me. Something I'd done that had gotten me in trouble. But what? I never found out because they never did come for me.

One spring day, when school let out, I stood in front of the building waiting for Carlo to walk me home. As the other kids ran past me, I saw my teacher, Sister Raymond, put her hand on Carlo's shoulder. He was looking up at her, nodding. Then they both turned and looked at me.

A shiver ran up my spine. Sister gently tapped his arm, and he ran toward me. My eyes followed him, and my heart raced. *Oh my God, I'm in trouble*, I thought, and swallowed hard.

When he reached me, though, he simply said, "Let's go."

I ran to catch up as he hurried past me. "What did Sister want?"

He didn't stop but said over his shoulder, "You did it now. Wait until Mommy hears." He continued to sprint, and I struggled to catch up.

"What did I do?"

He laughed and said nothing more.

When we reached our house, he climbed the steps two at a time, but I slowed down, defeated. I was as nervous as could be.

When I finally also reached the top landing, Carlo was talking a mile a minute to mom. She was smiling. Smiling? My eyes shifted to Carlo, and he too was smiling.

"You were selected to be a nun in the Mission Sunday Parade!" mom said, excited.

It was a special day for Catholic schools in the district. Everyone had been talking about it for days. I looked straight into Carlo's eyes, sure I should be angry, but I grinned from ear to ear, grateful and relieved.

Each October, the Catholic Church celebrated Mission Sunday. The observance had significant meaning for The Society of the Divine Word. Every parish was asked to have a special mass and collection for the missions. Each school was to choose two children, one boy and one girl to represent their parish and Order of Nuns.

I was chosen to represent OLS Dominican Order.

The day of Mission Sunday, I was taken to the Rectory where the nuns prepared me with the habit and headdress. They gave me a cookie and went to work. They greased my hair back to fit under the headpiece, which consisted of a white cotton cap called a 'wimple' that lay under a black bandeau of starched linen. It partially covered my cheeks and neck and extended down over my chest, like a bib. Then they pinned a black veil over the headdress, and lastly, a tunic of pleated black fabric was placed over my undergarments.

"Follow me," Sister said as she helped me off the table I was standing on. She took what remained of my cookie and placed it on the table. As I trailed behind her, I eyed the unfinished treat. I was sad to leave it there, knowing someone would come by and throw it away.

It was so delicious; I would have liked to have eaten it all. Silly as it was, I still think about that cookie.

Darlene on Mission Sunday as a nun, first nun behind Bishop boy

Before the parade was to begin, we were all brought to an auditorium to gather the parishes together. It was fascinating to look around and see miniature nuns, priests, and bishops. They showed cartoons and gave us huge rainbow lollipops. After a while, they finally called to us as the parade was to begin.

Not quite finished with my lollipop, I wasn't about to leave it there like my cookie. So, I wrapped it in a napkin. I remember seeing the nuns put their rosary beads inside a breast pocket that sat underneath the white bib, so I utilized it for my lollipop.

Spying my solution, two nuns approached me and asked how I knew about that pocket. "I see Sister Raymond resting her hand there, and all the Sisters use it for their Rosary." Amused at my explanation, they giggled, and we moved on.

Later, I learned not to wrap anything sticky in a napkin.

We were queued up outside, and when it was our turn, we began to march. People lined the streets on both sides. I saw dad in the crowd, smiling proudly, holding his camera up to get a few shots of me as I wobbled ahead, trying not to trip. I was a tiny little thing, but the wimple was tight to my face, making my cheeks appear chubby.

We made our way back around to OLS, and I was taken to the gym to wait for my dad. I had a great afternoon given all the attention I got that day.

TESSIE DOESN'T FEEL WELL

One night, when the house was still and everyone was asleep, Carlo called to me front my bedroom doorway. Anxious at the tone of his voice, I ran to him.

"What is it?" I asked.

"It's Aunt Tessie," he whispered.

"And?" I coaxed.

"She doesn't feel well," he said, feeding me slowly.

"What's wrong with her?" Concern rose in me. And for good reason.

"She's dead."

My eyes widened. "Dead!" I screamed in shock.

His delivery was not what I expected.

My sobs were loud and woke our parents. That's exactly what he didn't want to do. What he intended was to gently wake me up, tell me, then we could quietly tell our parents together.

Earlier, my grandparents had woken up Carlo because his bedroom was downstairs. They thought he could tell our parents without upsetting them too much. And, in turn, he thought he could wake me up and we could tell them together. Now, all hell had broken loose.

My parents came running, panic-stricken, out of their bedroom. My grandparents made their way up the steps as Carlo tried to stop my cries. With no control over the situation, I blurted, "Aunt Tessie is dead!"

More tears and shock. It was a night I've never forgotten.

It was a situation we now look back on and have a little laugh over. God rest Aunt Tessie. We still miss her, but laugh over how it all backfired for Carlo.

Aunt Tessie was my paternal grandfather's sister who lived in Ridgewood, Queens, not too far from us—just a twenty-minute car ride. I would take a drive with my grandparents once in a while to visit. She was a great cook and made Italian food beyond compare.

Everyone loved her because she was not the prim and proper lady that so many of my aunts were. She was boisterous, funny, cursed like a sailor, and had no filter. What I remember most about her husband, Uncle Al, were the Guinea Stinker cigars he smoked. They were small, thin, dark, and gnarly. Although small in size, they packed a punch of a pungent, acrid, nasty odor that made it hard to breathe. He used to sit in a La-Z-Boy chair and puff his smokes. He had a healthy head of grey hair, combed back and high. He wasn't much of a talker, not to my memory anyway, but he was a fixture in this spot of the living room.

They adopted a son, Albie. He had red hair, and his face wasn't what I was normally used to looking at in our Italian family. He had freckles and a crooked nose. He wore a leather jacket with chains on it, and his pant hems puddled at his boots. He had a collection of TV Guides. They were stacked up high in the corner of her living room that looked untouched for years.

Sadly, we lost touch with Albie after his parents both passed away.

ZOOZONDOO

Another Uncle, another unpronounceable name.

Zoozondoo was what it sounded like. Zio Santo was what it actually was.

He was married to my Great Aunt Virginia. She was my maternal grandfather's aunt, his mother's sister. Neither Zio or Aunt Virginia spoke English, so every conversation with them was solely spoken in Italian, of which I didn't understand.

Aunt Virginia lived in downtown Brooklyn in a Brownstone apartment. She was a strict, serious, take no bullshit woman. Even though we had a language barrier, there was no denying her temperament.

Like my grandmother and aunts, Virginia sewed for much of her life. She made lace doilies, curtains, aprons, and potholders. She had a Singer sewing machine and many colorful threads as well. They were of the thicker variety, called bonded nylon, and were sold loose so they hung down together like a wig would. Now, it's sold on a spool. She had some hanging from a knob on her hutch.

The glass door lay opened to reveal her teacups and saucers, but the threads were the thing that caught my attention. There were batches of many different colors. I have an attraction to anything colorful, and all I could think of was touching them. Too scared to act upon my urge, however, I also knew I couldn't get into Virginia's cabinet like I could Aunt Julia's office. The doors were bound together at the top, each color separated.

Which is why when opportunity knocked, I answered.

Grandma and Aunt Virginia were talking and drinking espresso, sipping from their pretty demitasse cups, so I went to the hutch, grabbed the threads, and plopped them on top of my head. I ran my fingers down the threads and swirled around and around, joyous.

When I stopped spinning, Aunt Virginia was staring down at me. "Questo bambino non ha buone maniere."

Frozen in my tracks, I placed the threads back on the knob. Grandma Laura was laughing, though, as she patted her lap for me to sit on. I ran past Aunt Virginia, who was giving me a sour look and didn't move an inch for the rest of our visit.

On the car ride home, I asked grandma what Aunt Virginia had said about me playing with the thread. "This child has no manners," she told me. But grandma said not to worry about her. "She's old and stuck in her ways, never had kids, so she has no tolerance." She waved her hand in the air to push the thought away.

As Grandpa Angelo drove, he agreed.

It wasn't so much that I enjoyed going to Aunt Virginia's house. It was more about getting out of the neighborhood for a few hours. It gave me something different to do. Besides, what could be worse than a mean ole aunt who doesn't let you touch anything? I'll tell you what, a ole uncle (Santo) who is so old, he just sits there not talking. And even when he did talk, I couldn't understand him anyway. He held an old vegetable can with the paper label torn off and spit into it. All. Day. Long. A can that housed his saliva.

All I could do was wrinkle my nose at the thought of his gross habit.

COTTON

I was afraid of cotton. I'm not sure why, and I never knew I didn't like it until I saw it—and then it was too late.

One night, I was coming out of the bathroom when I swung open the door and saw Joann holding something which was too close to my face to see. I stepped back from the white, fluffy substance. It came into better focus, and I didn't like it.

I ran back as far as I could as she chased me. I found myself behind the toilet. She was shoving it in my face, taunting me. The more I showed my fear, the more she shook it at me. Clearly, my options were running out, so I fainted.

As I lay crumpled behind the toilet, Joann ran to the medicine cabinet and reached for the smelling salts. She waved the open bottle under my nose, and I came to. Just as I got my bearings, though, she quickly jabbed the cotton back at me, and I disintegrated back onto the cold tile.

MY, YOUR CAT LOOKS DELICIOUS

My face was wrinkled in an angry expression. I wished Ralph had never came here from Italy.

He was Zio Antone's son. I didn't like him although I had no particular reason why. It was just my gut talking. He left his homeland, wife, and kids to seek work in America. Aunt Julia had graciously taken him in, so he lived with her in her small, one-bedroom apartment. He was able to share the fold-out bed with his father. It was to be temporary. Just until he found a job, then send for his family.

Ralph was eying up our cat, Rosie. He rubbed his hands together and licked his lips. He shifted his gaze from Rosie to me and back again. Rosie rubbed her face on the edge of the sofa and sprinted past me towards the bedroom. Ralph teased me and laughed with a strained, raspy throat that usually comes from smoking, as his did. He wasn't funny, but my father laughed along.

"They eat cats in Italy, and he wants to have him for lunch," dad said, chuckling.

Ralph said something back to him in Italian, and they shared a conspiratorial laugh.

He'd arrived from Italy only days before and was already planning a meal of Rosie over pasta? My expression must have signaled that I wasn't having it.

I ran from the room, unamused. I wished he would go back where he came from.

It would take another five months before he found work, thanks to my dad. He found a house just far enough away, in another part of Queens, and sent for his family. His wife and five children came, and my mom had a "Welcome to America" party for them. Unlike him, his family was nice, and I liked them all, but my feelings for Ralph never changed.

I must have held a grudge about Rosie, but she lived to see many years after that.

BUTTONS

Up until this point, I had never really seen the inside of a restaurant. Many a pizzeria, Italian deli, or hot dog stand, but nothing of the elegance of Lum's.

One afternoon, as Aunt Julia and I shopped around the Garment District in Manhattan, she asked if I was getting hungry.

"Um hum," I said, and she giggled.

We'd been busy all morning visiting fabric shops, looking at threads, buttons, and trim. The stores were so small, most of them cramped and narrow, with shelves full and overflowing. Navigating around was difficult, as I was told to hold her hand at all times.

We walked past brownstones with pretty iron window boxes. My favorites were the ones with vibrant red Geraniums spilling out. One lady was sweeping the sidewalk in her apron, and there was a delivery man ringing someone's bell with a tall stack of folded laundry. A young girl was walking six dogs at once—how hard that must have been!

The street was swarming with folks, it seemed alive, and once again, it made me feel good inside.

We came upon the store Aunt Julia wanted to go inside. It was four steps down from the sidewalk, and we had to open an iron gate first. There was a metal sign that swung from a stake in the ground that simply read, "Buttons."

A bell chimed as we entered, and when the door closed behind us, the sounds from the street were silenced. I followed Aunt Julia toward the back of the store, amazed at the amount of buttons I saw. There were shelves holding boxes upon boxes, some old and crushed from being pushed in and out over the years. Dust had built up that was never cleaned away. The writing on the cardboard was faded yellow and illegible. The front of the boxes had a sample of the button inside. Big ones, small ones, shiny ones, ones shaped like flowers, some like stars, half moons, and some plain, in every color and size imaginable.

Aunt Julia pointed to a few and decided on six different varieties. She asked for twelve of each variety. The lady was old and pleasant, but looked worn out and bored. She put each variety in a small paper bag, then all of them in a shopping bag.

We were off to lunch.

LUMS

What a treat, I thought. What was this place? White linen table-cloths, big vases with fresh flowers, shiny silverware, waitresses in uniforms. People dressed up in their best, fanciest, clothes. Candles lit on every table with a small vase of flowers. The staff zooming and sideswiping one another as they rushed past holding trays full of plates with steam rising up.

We were seated and given menus that were much too large and hard to navigate. Again, as she usually did, Aunt Julia giggled.

"Do you want a tuna sandwich?"

I nodded shyly.

When our food arrived, and my dish was placed in front of me, I could hardly see over it.

Aunt Julia smiled, enjoying my facial expressions. "Eat what you can," she said.

I took the fancy toothpick out and stuck it in my pocket, then un-hinged my mouth to take a bite. Not only could I not finish it all, three bites in and I was grabbing my stomach, shaking my head to signal "no more." Funny though, when the chocolate cake arrived, I found room for some, regardless.

It was obvious Aunt Julia got a kick out of me, and I loved her dearly. She was so special to me and made me happy whenever we were to-gether.

GOODBYE DEEDOO

Uncle Jack was sick and laid up in the hospital, yet everyone at home continued their daily routines. My siblings and I went to school, mom cleaned and cooked. Grandma Laura would meet us in the vestibule to unlock the door when we got home from school.

"Zio Antone passed away," she said one day as she let me in.

"You mean Uncle Jack," I corrected.

"No, Zio Antone died today, in the house."

I was taken aback. I stopped in my tracks. "What happened?"

She told me he hadn't been feeling well, so he went upstairs from the sewing room to lie down. Aunt Julia and grandma went up to check on him, and he gave one last breath.

We were all shocked at the news, and then, only a few days later, Uncle Jack also passed away.

It was a time of change. Nothing would ever be the same again.

Without so much as a word to me, Aunt Julia moved out. She went to live with Ralph, Zio Antone's son, and family. I was told only that. My heart broke to see her so sad, but mostly my heart hurt to see her go.

She didn't say goodbye. Maybe she couldn't bear it. We were like her kids, too. She went away to live with a new family and different kids, albeit our cousins, but I wanted her back.

The sewing room was eventually emptied and cleaned out. The basement was now just a basement. As time went on, I thought, she became more a part of them and less a part of us. I missed her terribly and didn't understand the reason she had to go until many years later.

Grandma and grandpa visited her from time to time, and when I could, I went too. They brought her groceries and an envelope with money to help her out. Ralph's wife would make pizza and spinach wheels. But as grandma and grandpa got older, they visited her less and less.

After I got married and had kids, I told them about her and how much I loved her. I decided to write to her, expressing my love for her and the heartbreak I felt when she went away. To my surprise, she wrote back and told me how sorry she was. She didn't realize how it affected me. She said she'd been grieving and had to go. There were too many memories, and it hurt too much to stay.

Ralph and his family took great care of her. She said she loved me and that I was special to her.

She sewed my kids dolls and gave them to us when we finally had a chance to visit. We wrote to one another for a while. She looked forward to my letters, and I looked forward to hers. For a time, we reconnected and told each other how much we meant to one another. She was a true warrior, living with only one kidney, and years later, breast cancer.

She was a champion to me. Not only a tender and sweet woman, but a peaceful, loving woman who touched my heart like no one ever had before.

She passed away at the age of ninety-seven.

THE NAME MAKER

"It's a quill!" mom would say when she was cold. At times, she'd blurt out, "Ishkabibble!" Not too long ago, I found out that means, "Don't Worry," and that it was the stage name of someone on a radio show in the 30s whose real name was Merwyn Bogue.

Mom referred to my dad as "Doolala." At some point, this must have rubbed off on my sister, Joann, who took this idea and ran with it. She called our brother, Carlo, "Curl." I was "Nook-a-foose." She called our younger brother, "Woose-a-soon-a thoon-a foose" or "Woosie" for short.

I have a strong suspicion the "Foose" was our last name.

When her boys were born, she called her oldest, "Fa-qua-e-que-etta-ensenta" or "Momuetta." Her youngest was "Mig-alear-lou-lottsa." And she wasn't finished yet. When my daughter was born, she was dubbed, "Welinga Welampus."

My dad had his own style, you could say. He was more of the 'you shouldn't say that' kinda guy, but he had the habit of calling my mother "Cock." Even weirder, my mom had a habit of answering to it. She didn't even resemble a rooster—or the other kind.

Unfortunately, he was not referring to a rooster.

Dad had no filter, and it was normal to us. I hadn't realized the enormity of it until I was in an elevator with these two nuts.

John and I were on vacation with my parents. It was the mid-'80s, and I had been married about one year at the time. I was twenty-seven years old. The four of us stepped onto a crowded elevator to go to dinner when my dad, the genius, who turned to mom and said something, then added, "Okay, Cock?"

I closed my eyes tightly and held my breath.

"Okay," she answered.

When the elevator doors opened, I was about to burst. I looked at my embarrassed husband and my clueless parents. "Mom, he called you 'Cock' in a crowded elevator!" She looked at me, not knowing what to say. "And you answered him!"

Her face showed that she thought about it for a second, then threw her head back and laughed.

Dad had a grin on his face, completely satisfied with himself.

CORONA NY, 11368

At fifteen, we moved to Long Island, against my power, my will, and my heart. I wasn't comfortable with change, and there was talk of moving. Mom and dad had started house hunting on weekends. My stomach hurt just listening to them tell my grandma about it. I felt like everything I knew would be pulled from under me. My comfort and security would be gone.

Leave Corona, I couldn't imagine. How would I fit in somewhere else when I barely felt like I fit in there? Shea Stadium was within walking distance from our house. When we looked out of the front window, we could see the flags flying from the bleachers of the stadium. If the Mets had a home game, we could see the bright lights and hear the accordion music echo through the streets.

Shea opened in 1964, the same year as The World's Fair, and they sat adjacent to each other for one year. Although Shea stood for forty-three years, the Fair was taken down in 1965. Shea was eventually demolished by a wrecking ball in 2008, rebuilt, and renamed Citi Field.

I don't claim to be a baseball fan, but it will always be Shea to me. Part of my home and heart.

There were so many places I would miss. The Lemon Ice King, which is still in business and thriving and a Corona staple. Walking to OLS every day, we passed Louis Armstrong's pink house. These were just a few of the many things that made living in Corona a sweet little place on the planet for me.

Paul Simon, who was born in Corona, even sang about it in "Me and Julio Down By the Schoolyard."

When my parents finally found a house and the signing commenced, the packing and the heartache began for me.

LONG BEACH, 11561

Moving from a borough in Queens to a suburb on Long Island was a culture shock to me.

I was fifteen and just beginning high school before we moved. I was unleashed from eight years in a strict Catholic school to a public school in Flushing. I had to take the train and walk about a half mile. I felt free and grown up. It was the first time I was allowed to travel alone.

Flushing High School was in a beautiful building. It was Gothic style, had turrets and gargoyles and was built in 1912.

I attended from September 1973 to December 1973, only three short months.

In December, during Christmas break, we moved. I had only seen our new house once before because I refused to believe we would actually leave. When the day came, and everyone scattered to say their good-byes, mom found me at my best friend's house. It felt like it was the end of the world.

The house was packed and ready, except for my room. My sister helped me out and threw all my belongings into a box.

I had one more stop to make on my goodbye tour, and that was to my boyfriend. He lived around the corner from me and was three or four years my senior. I was forbidden from seeing him due to my age, but puppy love prevailed and we snuck around. We met when he had a party at his house. I dare not ask my parents if I could go, so I slept over at my best friend's house instead.

Joann lived in an apartment building close to Jack's candy store. Mom always let us have sleepovers. This night, however, I made the fatal mistake of calling mom to say goodnight and that I was going to bed. The only trouble was, it was eight o'clock at night.

She wasn't buying that for a second.

After we left to go to the party, my mom called Delores, Joann's mom, to check on me. Delores was unaware of the lie, so she told mom we weren't in bed, but at a party. Somehow, though, I don't remember getting in trouble for it, not even a mention from mom. She trusted Delores decision to let her own daughter go, so she never mentioned it to me. I also think, if she got dad involved, there would have been trouble. He would have come right over and taken me home.

That night, at the party, I danced and made a fool out of myself. Not because I was drinking, I wasn't. It was because I didn't know how to dance. I was twirling and using my arms. It was a sight! Regardless, I got to talk to one of the sons who lived there and we began dating. I liked him very much, even though I knew our age difference was a problem. I was fourteen years old, and he was eighteen. An adult and a child, by legal standards.

His parents were kind, welcoming and inviting, something my parents would be as well, if I weren't still a minor.

Little by little, it ate away at me that I was hiding behind my parents' backs. I wanted to tell them, but I was afraid to. One night, I wrote a letter to my mom and left it under my pillow. I told her that I liked a boy and wanted their permission to see him. I went to school, and when I walked home that afternoon, I was pensive and hesitant to see what awaited me. I walked slowly, and as I reached my block, I stood by a tree to get up the courage to face her.

After some time, I pushed ahead and stepped through the door.

She was busy in the kitchen. She said hello without looking at me. I put my books down and changed out of my uniform. We were called to dinner a few hours later.

I watched her without being obvious. My eyes darted up from my plate to see if I could read a reaction from her. She wasn't smiling. She was eating. Then, she cleaned up as we scattered into our rooms to do homework. I thought she'd say something, anything. But no, I went to bed that night disappointed that she'd leave me hanging.

A week had gone by, and every night was the same. I'd search her eyes for a sign, but she didn't give me any. I sadly gave up hoping she'd talk to me about it. Even if she said no, it would be an acknowledgement, so I could stop hoping.

Then, one morning, while I was still in bed, she came and sat by me. She said she got my letter and was afraid to tell dad. She told me she was going to talk to him and let me know. I felt the weight of the world lift off me, just for a moment, until I began to worry about what dad would say.

After she informed dad, which took some time, he told me I could see him under some circumstances. One of them was I was not allowed to go to his house. They owned a bodega grocery store across the street from their home, and I was to see him there or outside only.

Grateful to be allowed to see him at all, I abided by my dad's wishes.

Then came a lapse in judgement.

My boyfriend worked at his parent's store and had a break and wanted to go home for dinner. I walked with him to his house, and his mother invited me in. His sisters and aunts were there. The house was full, and I was enjoying myself. Then came a knock at the door, more like a fist pound. One of his sisters came rushing from the window and said it was my father.

I had to hide. I had to, or he would kill us all. Not literally, but I didn't want to see his wrath.

They put me in his mother's bedroom in a closet. I was shaking like a leaf. He was shouting and asked to see me. They told him I wasn't there. He looked around for a few minutes, then left. I ran out the back door and got home after he did.

He looked at me and said, "You better tell me where you were."

I lied, naturally, and denied I was there.

"Well, your friend Joann just confessed to me and told me you were in that house."

Oh my God, I thought. *What do I do now?* "I was there, dad. I was invited to dinner. I'm sorry."

His eyes widened, and he was almost foaming at the mouth, he was so angry. I was trembling. "You're never to see him again. You got that? If I find out you are seeing him, you'll be sorry, and he'll be even sorrier."

My best friend, also named Joann like my sister, in fact did not tell my dad I was there he tricked me into a confession I learned later. And that was the beginning of the hiding.

I was in eighth grade, and he'd graduated already and drove a car. He would pick me up from school to steal a few minutes together, then drop me off at the corner.

After I moved to Long Island, he would drive to see me once a week. We'd hang out at my friend's house after I got home from school, and I'd make sure to duck down if we drove anywhere. This went on for three years. But as time moved on, I was growing up and a long-distance boyfriend was not getting any easier.

In my last year of high school, I met someone I would someday marry.

Me (far left), my dad with Jacquelyn on his lap and my mother.

THE LATE BOY

The high school I went to was a pleasant surprise, not like most high schools I've heard about. It had an open campus where students could come and go as they pleased on their free periods. There was a smoking lounge in the basement with wall-to-wall benches and music piped in.

There was also something else going on just outside the lounge.

We were on the bay, and students would go outside to smoke pot. I wasn't a fan. Rarely did I go down there on my break, though eventually I took a job in the attendance office signing in the kids who missed the bus and got there late for various reasons. I also had to call the homes of every absent student.

There were many times the smokers just decided to cut school that day or a few classes. I sat at a small window and gave late passes to them to take to their next class.

Almost every day, this one boy came by late for class. Long, blonde wavy hair, usually wet from a shower, with a mustache and full of attitude. But not arrogant—maybe a little overconfident. He had a swagger and confidence that was attractive. We began to spend our free periods together and talked for hours.

Everyone assumed we were dating, but that wasn't true. Yet.

He had a girlfriend who had just moved away, though they eventually stopped seeing each other. He'd just moved from the Bronx, and I from Queens. He came from a school where he was the minority and was beaten up more times than he could remember. At one point, he needed a police escort to school for protection.

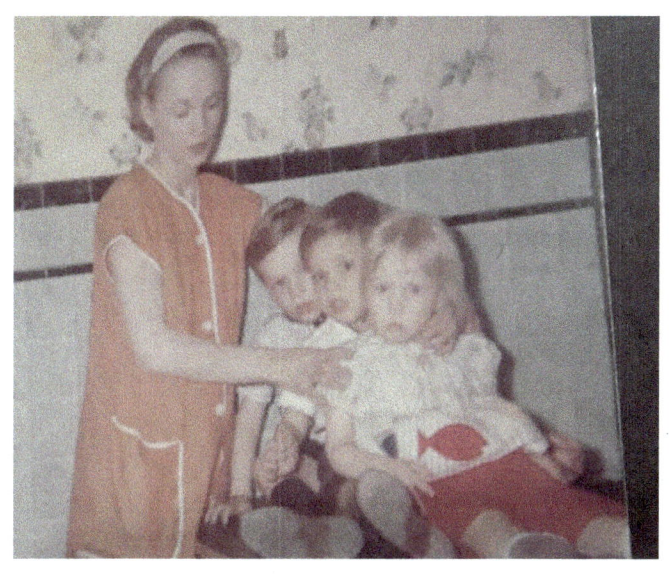

*My mother in law, Mary with my husband John in front of her
with his siblings.*

John and me 1977

His parents were divorced, and his mom had long since remarried. His dad helped his mom to buy a house on Long Island to get him and his other three siblings out of a dangerous neighborhood in the Bronx. They lived there a year prior to my family moving.

John had many girls wanting his attention, but I was oblivious to it. We grew closer and closer, and I thought it may be time to say good-bye to my first love.

A schoolmate called me one afternoon and told me I had a visitor at her house. It was my boyfriend. I knew I had to go, and I decided to call John and ask him to come with me.

I know, not the best idea.

When we got there, I could see he'd been crying. It hurt my heart, but I also knew he was seeing an Asian girl back home. Yet, there we were, ready to say goodbye, even though it was painful. He took me into another room and played me a song on his guitar. I was uncomfortable, but I indulged him.

He knew it was over.

He shook John's hand and left.

My father-in-law "Jackie"

John on his motorcycle

My daughter, her husband Jared, and my mom Joan at Jacquelyn's wedding.

My brother Joseph and his partner David (Joe is standing behind David).

My parents Joan and Carlo being silly.

My son, John pretending to hit Jacquelyn over the head with a rock.

Mom and dad being wheeled to the doctor's office by me with no other way to get them there together except to sit her on his lap.

Mom and Jacquelyn.

BEACH TOWN

It was the 1970s and being new to Long Island, you could tell the town was not rundown but quickly headed there. Our city was by the sea, and although the beach was beautiful, it didn't feel like home to me.

The hotels that were running horizontal to the boardwalk were dilapidated and housed by welfare recipients and the elderly. Government agencies were keeping patients who'd been released from mental institutions in the hotels. Sadly, they were basically left on their own with little to no help. They would walk around town, some muttering to themselves, others in bathrobes, some even walking into traffic. It was heartbreaking and sometimes terrifying to witness.

In the '80s and '90s, the city had urban renewal. The hotels were torn down and condos went up. New businesses opened, and the population grew. Of course, not only the population but also the price of buying and owning a house.

As time went on, I slowly forgot about my hometown and felt comfortable living in the suburbs.

OUR LIVES HAVE JUST BEGUN

John and I dated for eight years before getting married in 1985. To say we had an easy life would be misleading. To say we stuck it out together, in good times and bad, in sickness and in health—well, yes, that we did.

We got a little apartment in Brooklyn. My brother-in-law's parents owned a four-family house, and one apartment was available. It was so nice to have our own place. We both worked in Manhattan. I worked at a brokerage firm in lower Manhattan and John at a high school as a maintenance man.

Every night, we'd cook dinner together and watch TV. We had friends over and saw my parents on the weekends.

After three years, I got pregnant with our daughter, Jacquelyn. I worked at the brokerage firm for almost ten years, up until my seventh month of pregnancy. I was exhausted from walking six blocks to the train and then standing most of the way. John and I talked about it, and I decided to give myself an early maternity leave.

I put my notice in with my boss. And the plan of having two months off turned into one month because I had her early.

At the time, we were taking Lamaze classes to learn how to breathe during labor and for my husband to be able to help me focus on the breathing and not on the pain. Often, we had to face each other and do these very weird sounding breaths. Like two kids, we couldn't look at each other without completely cracking up.

The teacher made us do it back to back after that. So much for maturity.

John and me at our wedding.

Considering how painful giving birth can be, mine wasn't too bad. Yes, it was painful, but she arrived after only four hours of heavy labor.

My water broke the night before, but I don't consider it labor until it hurts. John had had a few drinks, and I was tired and went to bed. I couldn't sleep, though as I was too uncomfortable. So, I went to the bathroom and saw that I had a bloody show, signaling labor.

I called to my snoring husband, and he said, "Come to bed."

Then, water gushed from me, and I shouted louder, "My water just broke!"

Silence.

Snore. Snore.

"John, my water broke!"

"It's not from that."

Oh, really? Hmm, okay.

I called my sister, and she was so excited. I wasn't. I was scared out of my mind.

I called my doctor next, and he told me he'd meet us at the hospital at 5:00 a.m. "Go have a glass of wine and get some sleep. It's gonna be a big day tomorrow."

Oh, yes, sleep.

No, that didn't happen.

My parents made their way over from Long Island and waited with my sister and her in-laws. I have to admit, when the contractions started, it was intense. There was nothing but sweet relief when they stopped. John always had his eye on the monitor and could tell me before I was about to have another contraction.

Maybe that wasn't a good idea.

I was so dehydrated, but they only offered ice chips.

When she finally crowned, I screeched.

"Shhh, don't scream," the doctor and John said simultaneously. How I wish I could have captured my face in that moment.

"It's a ... it's a ..." The doctor said as he pulled her all the way out. "A girl! What are you naming her?"

"Jacquelyn," I replied.

It turns out the assisting nurse's name was Jacquelyn, too. It was a wonderful day and a beautiful memory—and the best thing I ever experienced.

I had my daughter in October 1988. I was thrilled to be a mother. The best feeling in the world. Yet, I was suffering from severe depression, doom, and anxiety.

Not knowing what was wrong, I kept it to myself because I couldn't describe what I was feeling. I didn't know where it was coming from or why. What I had didn't have a name at the time, but years later, it was called Postpartum Depression—along with anxiety attacks, which at the time were both undiagnosed in me, especially the postpartum. That's because it was typically never heard of before. This was 1988, and at the time, there was no internet. Information was difficult to come by.

According to Wikipedia, in the 19th century, gynecologists believed that female reproductive organs were at fault for "female insanity." Approximately 10% of asylum admissions were connected to "puerperal insanity," which is the period of about six weeks after childbirth in which a mother's reproductive organs return to their normal condition. It wasn't until the onset of the twentieth century that the attitude of the scientific community shifted once again: the consensus amongst gynecologists and other medical experts was to turn away from the idea of diseased reproductive organs and instead towards more "scientific theories" that encompassed a broadening medical perspective on mental illness.

But there I was, thinking I was dying or something dreadful would happen.

The cure was going home to my mother and being surrounded by my family where I felt most secure.

After some months of being back home, I began to feel better. My dad grew a strong bond with Jacquelyn, and I could feel myself relax a little. John came home from work and soothed her to sleep with music. Mom and I would go out every day with the baby while the men were at work. I loved being back on Long Island. Taking walks with her in the stroller and looking at the pretty lawns up and down the block.

Driving everywhere is also a convenience you soon appreciate when you're living in the city and have to travel by bus or train everywhere you go.

When Jacquelyn was a year and a half, we—or rather I—wanted a bigger place to live, but the only place we could afford was back in Brooklyn. I was about six months pregnant with our son at the time.

My sister once again found me a great apartment a few blocks from where we'd lived before. It had three bedrooms, a dining room, and a huge living room. The landlord was the sweetest woman. It was a two-family building, and she lived downstairs with her husband and daughter, who was about six years old.

I made friends with the girl next door, who was also pregnant and having a baby around the same time as I was. Oh, and we had the same obstetrician. But it didn't take long for me to realize what I'd done. I regretted moving back the minute the last box was placed in the kitchen.

Jacquelyn ran around the empty apartment the whole day. She ran in and out of closets and between our stacked-up boxes. After it got dark and we settled in, she looked at me with those big brown eyes and said, "Mommy, I want to go home now."

John stopped what he was doing and looked at me. I had tears along my lashes and looked him straight in the eyes and said, "So do I."

We let the moment pass, though. I was determined to stay.

I made the best of it until I felt the pull of home again. My delivery was pre-arranged. The doctor wanted me in and said he would determine if I needed a cesarean. He said the baby was too big to fit and that he'd induce me.

Mom and Dad came to babysit Jacquelyn, and we quietly woke up at 4:00 a.m. to leave for the hospital. I remember kissing her goodbye while she slept. We were never away from one another, not even for a day. I would miss her. I kissed her face a hundred times until John reached for my hand to tug me away.

I thought four hours of labor was fast, and although this delivery was scheduled, our son decided he was ready regardless.

My water broke on the way to the hospital. No cesarean necessary.

As I was in the delivery room, the nurses' shifts were changing and there was no one monitoring me, but my old, reliable husband. I told him I was nauseous, so he found a nurse who asked me to lie on my side.

She left.

John grew concerned as he looked at the baby monitor. It showed the heartbeat was diminishing.

He ran out into the hall and came back with the doctor and a nurse. They quickly moved me to a flat position again and the baby's heart rate went back up.

As I began to deliver, the doctor realized the cord was around his little neck. His voice was firm and strong, "Stop pushing!"

Oh dear God, how do I stop pushing? I tried with all of my might, but I couldn't stop. He still sliding out of me, and there was silence. I laid back and closed my eyes. I was a complete mess. Praying softly, waiting to hear him cry, I heard nothing. I couldn't open my eyes. I wouldn't open my eyes. Tears spilled down my cheeks like a river.

Then the doctor said, "It's a boy!" And I heard him cry!

Every part of my body relaxed, and I was flooded with more joy than I can describe. My little miracle boy.

His birth was traumatic and exhausting. I continued experiencing labor pains even after, something I'd heard is very common after the baby is born in subsequent births.

Soon my sister and mother brought Jacquelyn to see us at the hospital. She was screaming, "Where are you baby John?" as my sister held her, prompting her to continue.

Going through these feelings was difficult enough. I had a baby to care for. I couldn't stay in bed under the covers all day no matter how much I wanted to. Just putting one foot in front of the other to do everyday tasks were debilitating. Suddenly not working, not getting dressed up, traveling to work, laughing with co-workers, or scurrying around the office was a change in my life that had me wondering who I was. I felt my identity slipping away.

Sadness and anxiety. Panic and doom. My hands would shake, and I couldn't take care of my babies properly. I wanted to sleep. Close the blinds and keep the apartment dark. If Jacquelyn made noise, I'd yell at her to keep quiet. I hurt now when I think about that. How can you keep a two-year-old and a newborn quiet? You can't. They shouldn't be quiet.

I didn't know what to do.

One day, while visiting my grandparents, my Grandpa Angelo noticed I wasn't right. He asked me about it, and I didn't know myself. I blurted out that I was sad and lonely in Brooklyn.

He and Grandma Laura lived in my mom's house in the basement apartment. Often, I would drive them to doctor appointments or to go shopping when I lived there. Mom didn't drive, so I was their only help.

He told me I needed to be home with all of them. I knew he was right. I needed them, and they needed me. I wanted desperately to move back.

Turning to my mother, he said, "She needs to come home."

I looked at mom, and she said, "I'll ask your father."

I was a little taken aback by her response, but out of respect for the man of the house, I understood. Not the way I would have handled it, if it were my daughter, but mom was mom.

A few days later she said dad would love to have us back.

The first time we lived there, he'd grown a special bond with Jacquelyn. He was heartbroken when we moved out. Moving back home made me feel safe, stable, and happy.

We emptied the apartment, loaded up the car, and made trip after trip just John and I, with a little help from his wonderful Aunt Francis. And this time, we stayed put. We raised our kids, and I took deep pleasure and gratitude for having been able have our children live with two generations of family.

Me and John

A TIME TO FORGET

Settling into a new high school didn't fill me with joy. I'd already gotten used to Flushing High School and traveling by train like a grown up, and now there I was, expected to get on a yellow school bus to go to class.

To me, a yellow school bus was for children in grade school. I was in high school and wanted to feel mature, not like a child waiting on a corner for a yellow bus to pick me up.

I expressed to my mother that I was embarrassed, but my choices were get on the bus or get on the bus. So I got on the bus.

I was no different than any other student. We all waited in the freezing cold at 7:00 a.m. on our designated corners for the :baby bus" to arrive in all its noxious fumed glory. With every stop, it was more insufferable.

I'd stare out the window, wishing the day was over before it began. I felt out of place. I didn't belong there. The deafening chatter, the high-fiving and energy level at that hour of the morning was unbearable—where was all this enthusiasm coming from?

I wanted to go back to bed. Back to Corona. Back to the familiar.

The culture was different. The way they dressed was different. Even the way they spoke. Only a thirty-minute car ride away from where my heart belonged, yet such a difference. City life was in my blood, and this suburban atmosphere was both boring and strange to me.

Several months had gone by, and I needed a few books from the library, so I got off the school bus a few blocks before my stop. After checking out the books I needed, I walked home the rest of the way.

I saw a girl from class, and she introduced me to her brother as we continued to walk in the same direction. After a while, she turned off into a side street as her brother and I continued on. It was idle talk when he stopped in front of an apartment building and said he needed to run up to his friend's place to grab something. He asked me to go with him. Not thinking anything of it, I agreed.

It was several flights with no elevator.

When we walked into the apartment, he immediately threw me onto a foldout bed. I pushed him, trying to get away, but he laid on top of me and pinned me down. He might as well have been a boulder. I couldn't move. I fought every step of the way, and when he was done assaulting me, I ran down the five flights of steps, shaking and crying.

He chased behind me, apologizing profusely.

Once outside, I ran as fast as I could all the way home. Ashamed and embarrassed, I spoke to no one and curled up on my bed. I never thought of telling a soul. In some way, I felt I could have done something to stop him. At the very least, I could have said no to him and not went into the apartment.

I never even knew his name.

I didn't tell his sister when I saw her at school for fear she wouldn't believe me. I felt used and disgusted. I felt violated and intruded on. Those feelings stayed with me, and I was in a dark, low place for a while. Eventually though, I began to forget about it, or at least I put it away in the back of my mind.

I remember watching Oprah one afternoon and she had a show about rape. She mentioned that either someone was raped or knew someone that had been. I thought to myself, I was never raped. Then, as the show went on, I had an eye-opening moment.

Yes, I was raped.

Oh my God, I was raped. Why had I not known that? Why did I not associate what happened to me with being raped?

Oprah had a therapist on who explained that some women don't even realize it, and that was me. A traumatizing event that I didn't name. Maybe it was a protection mechanism.

That word alone is too much to handle. It is a violent act that takes something away from you that you can never get back.

Years later, I decided to tell some of my siblings and my husband. I was surprised at their reactions. I told them individually, but not a whole lot was said in response. After thinking about their reactions, I realized, what could they possibly say? They listened and stood quiet for the most part. But what do you say to someone who tells you this?

THE GREATEST LOVES OF ALL

Being a mother is an indescribable joy. If nothing else, it's the reason I'm on this planet. There's no greater bond and no greater responsibility than raising children. It's the hardest job and the most gratifying.

A mama bear, yes, always. They are the loves of my life, and I'm so grateful to have such beautiful children, inside and out.

Something inside of me was fulfilled when I became a mother. I read somewhere having children is like watching your heart walk outside of your body. This resonated with me because I have a hard time expressing what it's like for me to be a mother.

It's a sacred gift. An honor, a privilege, and a blessing.

Jacquelyn, my firstborn, is everything a daughter should be. She is kind, thoughtful, empathetic, and funny. She cares about this earth and all human rights. I don't recall having an argument with her that ever went beyond a minor disagreement. When we are together, we can talk for hours or be comfortable in silence. We laugh at the same things, have many inside jokes, and just get one another without saying a word.

My son, John, was born two years and one day after my daughter. He's quiet, intelligent, and has integrity. He's hilarious and makes me laugh like no other. He gives me great advice and cares deeply.

I have great respect for them both and trust their judgment and advice. There's nothing I would not do for them.

John Joe

Jacquelyn, John and Koko

Me and my adult kids.

Baby Ja's cardboard doll house.

A MOMENT IN TIME

Nothing lasts forever, not even a nightmare.

How you get through hardship depends on your attitude. It's easy to have a good attitude when things are going smoothly, but your test begins when it hits the fan.

I felt a lump on the side of my right breast and decided to see the doctor. I was too afraid to tell him, so I waited for the exam for him to notice. He began examining me and froze when he got to the lump. I closed my eyes and held my breath.

My mother and the kids were in the waiting room.

The doctor was concerned at not only the size of the lump but also the ripple the skin had. It was a bad sign. He told me to go straight to the hospital. The kids were singing and dancing around me, and I felt faint. They put ice on my pulse points and let me rest until I could drive myself there.

I was thirty-four years old. Jacquelyn was six and John, four.

As I lay on an exam table at the hospital, I was dizzy and wanted to throw up. Doctors and nurses came out of every door to witness the lump themselves. A doctor leaned into toward me when I whispered, "I'm frightened."

He looked me in the eye, and said, "You should be."

I never forgot his face or his name. He's still a breast surgeon in town. I prayed for the women who came after me who had him for a doctor. I laid back and closed my eyes.

The following week, that doctor did my biopsy and after waking up, he told my husband and I that he wished he had better news for me, but that I should get my life in order because the statistics weren't good. We were devastated, and I was too weak to cry.

The only thing I was thankful for was that the anesthesia hadn't worn off yet, so I could sleep.

The doctor went to the lobby to find my mother. He told her the bad news. She screamed, "She has two kids! What am I going to do?"

The doctor shook his head and left her there. I found out later about this exchange when my sister told me. It left me shaken and heartbroken. My mother was thinking I would die and that she would have to raise my kids—that was a hard pill to swallow.

The family was called, and everyone supported me on this journey. My brother, Joe, found me a wonderful doctor in Manhattan and everything changed for the better after that.

It was a day that changed my life. The sun was shining again, and I was on my knees thanking God for my brother and Dr. Gaynor, my two heroes.

The doctor told me he was seeing younger and younger patients with breast cancer. He told me the type of cancer I had was fast growing and aggressive. He said that five years prior, there was no cure but that he had a recipe that I must follow. To see every step through, no matter what. Even if I was eventually declared cancer free, I had to do all the steps.

The first was to get tests to make sure it didn't spread. That very day, my brother and his friend Ray, John, and I took a cab to every doctor appointment set up by Dr Gaynor. He asked each doctor if they could see me that day. I was grateful that Dr Gaynor did this, or I would have had to keep traveling to the city for each separate appointment. I had my heart checked and a stomach ultrasound. I was even tested to make sure my heart was strong enough to endure chemo and a body scan, which was intense for me.

I had to stand up in front of a machine and be still. The machine began at my feet and worked its way up to my head. It turned me a little and did the same thing over and over again until my entire body was checked.

When I was done, the doctor came into my changing cubical and asked me not to get dressed yet. He said to sit and wait while he checked the scan. My hands clenched tightly together. I sat waiting, thinking of my babies at home. I just wanted to be home, breathing them in. My strength comes from them. They kept me going.

The curtain opened, and the doctor smiled. He held out his hand to mine. I shook it. "Congratulations, you're all clear and free to go!"

I smiled and thanked him, got dressed, and ran out into the awaiting arms of my husband and brother. I shared the good news, and we were on to the next appointment.

Dr. Gaynor said I'd begin with a round of chemo, two weeks on and two weeks off. Then, after two months of that, I'd have a radical mastectomy, followed up by a bone marrow transplant and radiation. They harvested my own bone marrow because it was healthier than needing a donor.

Small miracles began to happen.

ADRIAMYCIN

My chemo began in the summer of 1994. It was a drug called Adriamycin. It made me nauseous and my pee red. I never threw up after chemo because I took anti-nausea meds.

The scary part was the not knowing, but once we had a plan, I felt much better. I give all the credit to Dr. Gaynor. He was born to be an oncologist, a giant among doctors. He told me he would cure me, and I believed him with all of my heart.

On chemo days, my husband drove me to Manhattan. I would see mothers pushing strollers and felt homesick.

"I miss my babies," I'd tell John. He would reach over and squeeze my hand.

I saw everyone rushing about. Were they complaining about the chores they had to do or the places they had to be? Were they stuck in traffic cursing out the world? Did they know how lucky they were? Would they change places with me? I'd give anything to have a mundane life. What was it like to be normal? I'd forgotten.

The world went on even though I had cancer, and I was missing my babies.

Everything kept going just as it always had, but for me, everything was different.

The weeks I had off of chemo were some of the sweetest memories. I would lay on the floor and play board game with the kids. We would sing at the top of our lungs and laugh at stupid jokes.

I lived in each moment and didn't focus on what was next.

HAIR TODAY, GONE TOMORROW

"The watusi juice is working!" Andreya said excitedly. My oncology nurse expertly and gently pulled the needle from my arm and cleaned the area with a cotton swab. She looked me over and smiled. "You cut your hair." I grimaced and nodded. I ran my fingers over my scalp. "When your hair falls out, that means the watusi juice is working."

The watusi juice she referred to was the chemo, and when I started finding clumps of hair on my pillow, John took me to my salon to have them shave my head. The girls there knew me and knew what was going on. It wasn't too hard for me to do, as I put it in perspective.

Logically, I knew it would grow back. I knew I had much bigger issues ahead of me than a bald head. I also knew I was about to lose part of who I was.

I stared straight into the mirror and watched. First, she put my hair in a ponytail and cut it off. She would check in on me once in a while. My husband was right there beside me the whole time, too.

The other girls in the salon were kind and supportive.

She began to cut my hair, and then it was time for the buzzer. My eyes stung and tears welled up quickly. John came closer and held my hand. When she was done, they all hugged me and told me I looked good bald. My eyes were beginning to have dark circles around them, and my skin had a yellowish tint—and now, with no hair, I was a walking poster child for someone battling cancer.

WIGGED OUT

I was never a hat person, but I had to reconsider now. My parents offered to buy me a wig, and we went to a place who specialized in women with cancer.

After trying on a few, I found one that closely matched the color and style of my hair. We put it in a ponytail, and it was even more of a match for me.

It was still warm in early October, and the wig made me feel like I was suffocating, so at home, I wore a hat.

I drove to pick my son up from Pre-K and buckled him in. We stopped for a red light, and I leaned over and asked him for a kiss. My head hit the top of his Power Ranger baseball cap, and he started to giggle.

"What's funny?" The light changed, and I drove on. John was still laughing. "What? Tell me, come on."

He was a quiet kid, and I knew he wasn't going to tell me, so I glanced in the rear-view mirror instead. My ponytail had turned to the side and looked like it was coming out of my ear.

I gasped, "Oh no!" But then I started laughing too. I grabbed my ponytail and twisted it back around.

My sweet, funny four-year-old always found a way to keep me laughing.

A GOOD DAY FOR GOOD NEWS

After my first round of chemo was over and I was going back and forth from my oncologist to the breast surgeon, my radical mastectomy was scheduled for September 19th at Beth Israel Hospital in Yorkville on the East End of Manhattan. I'd never been to that hospital before.

It was across the street from Gracie Mansion, where the mayor lived.

My stay would be a short one, and I had the best doctors and felt safe. My roommate was a beautiful Jamaican woman named Novelette. Not only did I love her name, but I could listen to her talk all day. She had an ongoing health issue but nothing life threatening—thank goodness

The day after my surgery, I was bandaged up, but the nurses encouraged me to have a walk around for exercise, so I often took strolls back and forth on the floor I was on. I had a magnificent view of the East River. I sat on the windowsill sometimes; the warm sun felt good on my face.

I closed my eyes and took a moment to thank the universe for all the good I was receiving. The surgery was behind me, but the pathology report wasn't in yet.

I heard someone walking down the corridor and opened my eyes to smile at her. She was a nurse and looked radiant as she spoke to me. "I heard the news, congratulations!" I didn't know her but assumed she was in the operating room that my surgery had been performed in.

"Thank you." I walked back to my room and found my surgeon, Dr. Cahan, waiting for me.

I sat in bed, and he said he was delighted. "Textbook. Surgery went well, and I have high hopes for you."

After getting that wonderful news, a while later, Dr. Gaynor came in and sat with me. I hadn't told him Dr. Cahan had already told me. I felt he had a right to tell me, too.

"Your pathology report came back, and you're cancer free."

I put my prayer book down and laid my hands over my mouth. That was even better news than I'd expected.

The best news I could hear came from the best doctor on the planet.

SPARK PLUGS

Deep into the second round of chemo, it was taking a toll on my veins. They inserted a catheter. Another surgery. A thin, flexible tube was inserted into my chest so they could administer the chemo without having to find a vein that was not collapsed.

A nurse came over several times to show my husband how to clean the tubes so I wouldn't get an infection. My husband was quick to learn, and did it better than anyone else. He's the kind of guy you want next to you in an emergency. He's the guy that stayed with me through it all.

I will be forever grateful for the way he took care of me and has always cared for me.

Soon, it was routine to clean up dinner, give the kids a bath, shower, and get ready to have my "spark plugs" cleaned. The kids knew when I said, "spark plug time."

After each chemo, I needed a shot in my leg for two nights in a row, and of course, John would do the deed. My babies would give me all the support they could, too, though. Jacquelyn was a little scared and John Joseph, at four years old, stood next to me and held my hand.

"You're so brave, and I feel so safe now." I would give him a kiss and thank him. I would tell Jacquelyn when it was done, hug her and tell her she was very brave too.

THERE'S ALWAYS ROOM FOR LAUGHTER

My sister and brother-in-law stopped by the hospital to see me and brought some prank gifts to cheer me up. Glasses with eyes on a spring, and other fun items. She told me mom and dad were just getting off the elevator, so I grabbed the eyeglasses and took my hat off to reveal my bald head.

I sprang out of bed. "I'll be right back."

They followed me into the hallway as I began walking toward the elevators. I put the silly goggles on, and the spring made them bounce as I walked. I began feeling around the air as if I couldn't see. My bald head made for a great final touch.

I saw mom and dad headed toward me. They didn't recognize me. As I felt my way ahead, we were just about to pass each other. She had a scared look on her face and moved out of my way. I took my glasses off, and Joann and Angelo laughed behind me.

"Oh my gosh, I didn't know it was you! I thought, 'oh this poor girl,'" my mother said, also laughing.

They were surprised to find me in a playful mood after what I'd just been through. To me though, it was a great relief to hear I was cancer free. I couldn't have heard anything better. I knew I had to face much more treatment still, but today was a great day, and I wanted to be silly in that moment.

TRA LA LA BOOM DE AY

One more round of chemo, and I would be half done with each step I had to take. I knew what chemo was now, and it wasn't the most horrible thing to endure. I imagined it going through my veins and sending healing throughout my body, not only the cancer, but every part of myself. I was happy and, probably for the first time in my life, relaxed and relieved.

Every part of my body was checked. I knew I was healthy now, even though I still had to go through a bone marrow transplant. I didn't know what that would feel like, but I trusted Dr. Gaynor with everything I had.

The kids, my husband, and I would play board games at night in the attic. My mom went to bed around 9:00 p.m. to watch TV. Her room was right below the attic steps, and she could hear me laughing. She said it was so good to hear because it sounded like it used to before the cancer.

"Tra La La Boom De Ay, I have no boobs today!" I'd sing and run after my kids with my hat off. They'd giggle, and my husband would shake his head and laughed at how silly I was.

I told my kids from the start that I had cancer. I told them I needed the best, strongest medicine to get better. I told them that the strong medicine would make my hair fall out, but that would be a great thing because it would mean I was getting better. They didn't seem afraid and accepted our new normal.

We did homework and studied every night. I read them a story before bed and tucked them in. Life was as normal as possible, and they were so brave—my true heroes.

LOPSIDED

I was one breast down and had a huge boob on my left side that made me feel uneven and lopsided. I had to keep getting mammograms every six months, and as my PTSD got worse, the closer my appointments would get.

Two weeks before, I stopped socializing, stopped answering the phone and waited for the day they would say my results were negative for cancer. I could no longer function knowing this was going to happen for the rest of my life, so I decided to have my healthy breast removed.

After some difficulty, I found a doctor in Manhattan who would perform the surgery. Most doctors wouldn't touch me because of my age and the chances of me getting cancer on the other breast were low. Higher than most women, but low for me. Dr. Gaynor put a call into a surgeon he thought would do it for me, though. He knew my nerves would leave me paralyzed with fear for the rest of my life otherwise.

The doctor agreed, and I was set for surgery.

Having a completely flat chest was so liberating, freeing, and joyful. My brother Joe told me to wear my scars as badges. They were something to be proud of, and I was beginning to see it that way. I enjoyed not having breasts for many years, but then, I started to want to feel complete again.

In 2004, I decided to have reconstructive surgery. As much as I loved the feeling of being free from breasts, I also found strapping on a bra and large prosthesis most uncomfortable. I found a great surgeon close to home and had a few consultations before going full speed ahead. I wasn't a candidate for implants because the skin on my right chest wall didn't have enough elasticity to place an implant, nor did I want any foreign objects in my body. So my only option was called a Tram Flap where they take the skin, blood vessels, and the strongest muscle from the stomach and move it up to the chest. He would put mesh over the muscle to hold it in place. I wouldn't have a very important muscle in my stomach anymore, making it difficult to sit upright or get out of bed without rolling onto my side, but it was a sacrifice I was willing to take.

Years later, I would joke about "What a mesh I was!"

Dr. Cooper, my reconstructive doctor, had to follow procedure and take photos of my chest from all angles. He brought me into a tiny room, accompanied by a nurse, and I had to undress down to my underwear. The lights were blindingly bright, and there were too many mirrors. Why they were there, I don't know. I had to stand in front of a white screen with my hands on my hips. This was embarrassing. Overweight, scars from here to kingdom come, standing in my underwear.

Well, out of sheer humiliation, I put my hands on my hips, and the doctor positioned his camera up to his face, when I blurted, "Who's the lucky fella who will develop these?" The doctor lowered his camera, and I could see him repressing a giggle, and the nurse was quietly laughing too. I broke the tension, and we continued on from there.

I asked him if I would be in pain after the surgery, and he said, "You'll have discomfort."

Okay then. I was ready.

Surgery lasted seven hours, and I looked like a mummy afterward. I was bandaged from my chest to my stomach. Dr. Cooper popped his head in to take a peek at me. I called him over.

"Remember when you said I would have discomfort?" He nodded. "Well, it's called pain. Just so you know, if anyone else asks."

I could swear he grinned, but then again, I was groggy from the anesthesia, and maybe he just thought I was joking like I had been in the past.

Either way, now he could tell his patients it was indeed painful, though I doubt he would.

A BREAK FROM PRE-KINDERGARTEN

The bone marrow transplant day was approaching. I would be in the hospital for three or more weeks. Dr. Gaynor couldn't say it could be more but probably not less.

I had to make sure I made a schedule for my mother on what to do while I was gone. Jacquelyn had gym on Thursdays, so she had to wear gym clothes with sneakers. Wednesday was Hot Dog day, so I put 50 cents in four envelopes with her name and preferences. I laid out her uniform, tights, and shoes. I asked mom to check her folder every day, as that was the only correspondence with the teacher.

My son's Pre-K teacher called us in for a meeting, and the principal was there too. She suggested we pull John out of school for December and January, just until I had the transplant.

"He's here, but he's not here," She explained. She noticed he was depressed and didn't want him coming to school 'kicking and screaming' while missing me while I was away. They thought it would be better for him to be home with his dad and grandparents for the time being.

They then called him into the room and asked in a gentle way if he would like to leave school until mommy gets back home from hospital. He nodded his head quietly, and we knew it was the right thing to do.

Three weeks was a long time for a child to wait. It was a long time for me, as well. We had never been apart for that long, and this would be the most difficult of anything I'd ever had to do. Although he was better off at home, in the safety of our family, he refused to play Power Rangers with grandpa and just sat by the window, waiting for me.

SAINT AGNES

My bone marrow was postponed because my insurance wouldn't cover the hospital stay.

One Sunday afternoon, my surgeon called me with the bad news. He told me not to worry, though. "No matter what, you're getting this transplant."

I was scheduled to go in right before Christmas and stay through New Year's, and I was okay with that—until it fell through. My husband was happy I'd be home for the holidays, and it worked out for the best.

In January 1995, my husband drove me to St. Agnes in Westchester, New York. The nurse said we could check in during the evening, if we wanted to.

Aside from the thoughts of what was ahead, I couldn't stop thinking of what I left behind. My whole heart was behind me, in a living room on Long Island where I left my babies. I missed them so much, it hurt. I wanted to dive into their arms and take in the smell of baby powder and soft skin. A lump formed in my throat, yet I pressed on.

John took a leave of absence without pay to take care of me and to help my mom with the kids. Without my parents, we would have had a difficult time with rent and the kids. They were my angels. Plus, my best friend picked Jacquelyn up for school each morning and dropped her off after. Her daughter and Jacquelyn were also best friends, and we all remain best friends today.

This transplant I was facing was the hardest of all my treatments by far. I tried to focus on one thing at a time. Dr. Gaynor told me to be present and just do what's in front of me.

From that day on, I had tunnel vision.

John dropped me off at the entrance and went to find parking. I sat in the lobby waiting for him and observed people coming and going, crisscrossing in my path. There was a man holding a bouquet of pink balloons with a euphoric expression on his face as he hurried to the elevators. How wonderful and exciting to welcome a new baby. I was suddenly reminded that a hospital was not only a place where bad things happened but where miracles happened too.

I lost myself for a moment in this stranger's world. My heart ached to be in that place again. The joy of having a baby is unlike anything else in the world. I got to live that miracle, twice. How lucky was I to have two healthy, wonderful children.

John came in through the revolving doors, and it snapped me back to reality. A bone marrow transplant was waiting for me.

I got up, and we found the admissions department to sign in.

Often, I would worry about my husband. What was he feeling? What was he going through? Was he scared? We didn't talk about it, we just carried on, and it was full speed ahead.

My sister told me he asked God why I got cancer and not him. He was a smoker and thought I didn't deserve this. It made me cry to hear he felt this way. No one deserves cancer, smoker or not.

I was brought to my room and happy to see I'd be alone. It was the quarantine ward. Once in there, whoever stepped in had to have on a gown and mask so I wouldn't get germs, as I would be more susceptible after the transplant took place.

John saw that I was settled, then told me he'd be back soon, and when he returned, he had dinner and small paintings, nails, and a hammer from the dollar store. He began to decorate my room so I'd feel at home. My heart was so grateful for him. Not because of the paintings, but because the thought of the things he did for me overwhelmed my soul.

We ate chicken cutlet "hero" sandwiches (as we call them in New York) then it was time for him to go. Fear rose in me. He hugged me goodbye, and I wanted to dissolve into his jacket and go with him. The last part of my heart was going now. I would be here alone, facing something for which I had no idea what was about to happen.

The hallway was still—no other patients but me. That's why the nurses let him come and go so freely.

I changed into a nightgown and robe. I put on my fluffy socks and pulled the sheets up to my chest. A nurse came in with a wheelchair and asked me to go for a ride. She brought me to the lowest level, "For a few tests," she explained. She parked me just outside a room and told me that someone would be with me shortly. I watched her disappear into an elevator.

The night brought with it a peculiar mood. There was a loud silence, and everything felt hollow. The smell from the laundered gowns that sat in a bin just next to me made me turn away. Faraway aromas from an earlier dinner service and the putrid smell of urine lingered in my nose while I'd been wheeled down. And the dull fluorescent lightbulbs lent an eerie coldness that could have been better thought out when they designed the area.

Brighter lights and some wall murals would have helped.

I watched the large clock high up on the wall, refusing to move its hands. I felt forgotten and wondered if anyone would show up.

I'd been alone many times before, but that was different. I was alone. Alone in a depressing hallway and alone in my disease. Yes, I had family and doctors, and each person was an integral part of my healing, but when it came down to it, it was my arm that felt the pinch of the needle, my veins that poison went into. Yes, chemo is a medicine, but it's also a toxin. I was the one being put under anesthesia and giving it all up. I was alone.

I gave it my all and hoped it would pay off.

Some told me I was brave, but in the end, what choice did I have? Brave was the only option. The only choice I did have was that I could wake up every day and be worried, or I could wake up every day and be grateful. I chose to be grateful.

A MIRACLE ON BEECH STREET

John's drive to see me every day was a long one. Long Island to West-chester was about an hour, one way. Once you reach the Hutch or Hutchinson River Parkway, there are a few tight curves to pass, and if your eyes are filled with tears, it makes it that much more treacher-ous. This was his daily routine. Alone in the car with his thoughts and worries.

He had two small children to look after and a very sick wife. He never showed worry or fear to me, but I knew when he was alone, all bets were off. We did have talks about it later on, so I was able to tell this.

He always drove a little over the speed limit, as we all do from time to time. One night, not too far away from the house, he was headed out of town to see me but got stopped for speeding ticket. He explained to the officer what was going on and the cop said that all he could do was tell him to explain it to the judge and hope he could get it reduced. The courthouse was in the small town he got the ticket in, and he had to go in the evening.

It was darker than usual because there weren't many street lamps. He made his way into the building and saw the clerk. He told her what happened, and she spoke to the judge, who reduced the ticket down to $100 from $150. They told him they'd accept small payments, and he left.

He was walking back to his car when someone came from behind him, calling to him. "Excuse me?" the voice said. My husband turned around to look at who was talking, but couldn't see his face. "I heard your story," The stranger said. He held out his hand to give John something. John took it, looked down at it—and there was an $100 bill in his hand. He looked back up to say thank you, but no one was there. He searched up and down the block and found no one. No slam of a car door, just silence.

He went home that night and told my mom, and she told him it must have been his guardian angel.

That wasn't the last of our miracles, as there were many more along the road to my recovery.

THE SMILEY CALENDAR

Preparing to be away from my kids involved a lot of details, but the hardest was keeping them happy in the meantime. Jacquelyn's principal had a good idea to give us each a calendar with smiley face stickers, and while we were apart, we would put a sticker on that day to show we were getting closer to me coming home again. I knew that was something that would be of great help to both of us, but after a while, Jacquelyn was showing signs of sadness. She'd sit under the dining room table, not want to get out of bed in the morning for school.

When John was able, he brought the kids with him to see me. They too had to abide by the rules and wear a mask, gloves, paper shoes, and robes.

The first time they walked into my room all covered up, and I saw their big eyes looking at me over their masks, it broke me. I was putting my innocent children through this scary time, and I had no way to protect or comfort them.

They sat on my bed and drew me pictures that later John hung on the wall. Falling asleep to those images made me feel loved and safe. Those drawings were precious reminders that I was loved, needed, and missed. Laying there, too weak to do anything, I'd stare at them and fall asleep.

SORROW AND REMORSE

During the bone marrow transplant, which took three days of intense chemo, I was heavily medicated, and my vision was impaired. I slept most of the time and never ate.

John brought the kids in one night, and I took one look at them and started screaming to get them out. That was so uncharacteristic of me.

Their sweet little faces were so disappointed. They drove over an hour to see me, and I yelled for them to go.

John took them home, and the next day, my mother called me and told me how horrible I acted and that I shouldn't have done it. I was already grappling with regret and anger at myself, though, so I cried at the thought of what I'd done. I didn't even know why I'd done it. I loved them more than life itself, and I hurt them.

I was a mess, and it was the biggest regret I'll ever have. I was not myself, and I will forever be sorry that happened.

My logical mind told me it was from being heavily medicated, and I'm sure, to this day, that is why. But my heart tells me it was the worst thing I've ever done to them. And in my soul, I won't forgive myself for it.

SHAKE AND BAKE

The morning after I was admitted, I was taken to surgery to harvest my own bone marrow. I was laying on a gurney, prepped and ready for the surgeon to arrive. Since my illness, I found myself time and time again observing people around me. It almost felt ethereal, as if I didn't exist, as though I was spying and they couldn't see me.

That morning, the nurses came in, one by one, and some gathered together, drinking coffee. They talked about TV shows and what was on the agenda for the weekend. One nurse had just bought a new pair of sneakers and was turning her foot from side to side, showing them off.

All the conversations, all the distractions and trivial things that kept our minds busy was now replaced, for me, with one thought—and that was cancer. I had an optimistic outlook, and I made the best of it, but forefront on my mind was cancer. There were no thoughts of sneakers or shopping. No thoughts of what I would do that weekend. I just wanted to be healthy and go home to my babies and husband.

I was given general anesthesia, then they inserted a needle into the cavity of my rear hip bone where a large quantity of bone marrow is. It was extracted with a syringe and frozen to be saved until the day of my transplant. That would be done to restart the growth of my bone marrow due to the extremely strong chemo.

The transplant took place at my hospital bed, and it was infused intravenously. I had to be monitored very closely for the next three weeks, which was a crucial period. The high doses of chemo destroyed my bone marrow and crippled my immune system. During this time, as I waited for the bone marrow to migrate to the cavities of the large bones and begin producing normal blood cells, I was susceptible to infection and excessive bleeding.

The doctors didn't say what could happen because there was no way to know. Everyone was different. We'd just take it moment by moment.

Every few hours, my temperature was taken, as I was running a high fever. They told me to click the morphine drip when I needed it, and I found myself clicking it even when it wouldn't give me more. On the last night of the transplant, my fever peaked, and I had convulsions.

The main thing I remember was shaking to a point that my body was jumping off the mattress. I was extremely cold, sweating, and shivering. The nurse soothed me to sleep by rubbing my back and whispering to me, "There now, it's okay." She kept leaving to get more blankets, but no matter how many she laid on me, I couldn't get the chill out of my bones.

She told me she was going to try and find a heated blanket, and after a long while, she found one and brought it to me.

My room was dark, only a sliver of light coming from the hallway. As she leaned in again, she told me she'd stay with me through the night. Sometimes guardian angels live on Earth too.

That night, I had seen the darkness—it was the worst night of my life.

Morning had come, and I was more alert than I'd been in days. I was in a happy mood when John came in, and I showed him the ice mattress I was laying on.

"Look at this," I said.

He twisted his feet around and was no sooner in my room, then he was out. Off to the nurse's station to ask why I was on an ice mattress.

They told him about my 'shake and bake' situation and how high my fever spiked. When he came back to the room, we didn't discuss it or about the night before.

When my fever finally broke, I was told I needed a blood transfusion. It was ten years after the AIDS epidemic, and I was concerned. John and I talked to the nurse who told us that my blood would be broken up into platelets and T cells, which were white blood cells that were of key importance to the immune system. She assured us that the blood was carefully tested and safe, but I had no choice anyway, so I had the transfusion.

Days had passed and looking out my window into a parking lot, all I remember was how much it rained. It seemed the whole of January it rained. I brought many books and magazines, thinking of how much reading I was going to do. It turned out, the nurses would sit in my room and read them instead.

After the infusion came an esophagus infection. If felt like a bad cold with phlegm, only it was phlegm from hell. It seemed to start down in the deepest depths of my windpipe. I tried to get it out, but it seemed to be tethered to my lungs, and no matter how much spitting up I did, nothing would bring relief. I even tried pulling it out with my hands. It was as if I was a magician, pulling scarfs out of a magic hat.

After a few days, I was given a tongue scrapper, which helped a lot. I asked why I didn't get it before. They said they wanted the body to begin healing itself first.

Once I began to produce normal blood cells, I was gradually taken off antibiotics and the blood transfusions stopped too. After three weeks, Jacquelyn and I had placed the last smiley face on our calendars, and I was released from St. Agnes.

The lady who cleaned my room said she wanted to wheel me down to the car, the nurses said they would do it, but my doctor's assistant, Elizabeth, told them she would do it—and so she did. It was bittersweet. I couldn't wait to go, but I would also worry that I wouldn't be monitored as carefully at home. I was weak and could hardly walk.

Recovery would take months.

I AIN'T LION

Dr. Ahmed is a brilliant, kindhearted, and gentle oncologist, who specialized in Stem Cell Transplants. He's Chief of Oncology and an expert in his field. He performed my stem cell transplant, and I feel grateful to him for saving my life. I was going to miss him as my three-week stay at St. Agnes came to an end.

Elizabeth, Dr. Ahmed's assistant and very involved in my care, was at the foot of my bed every single day along with him and a few interns. They'd be equipped with charts and clipboards as they analyzed my progress. They checked my test results along with my vitals and asked me questions about how I was feeling. I can't recall my answers, but many times I remember them laughing and getting a kick out of me. I don't know what I said in those times, but some things never change with me, as I like to make light of stressful situations.

I was petrified of Dr. Ahmed, but only because I was always worried he'd bring me bad news. I got over it after a while, discerning that wasn't the direction of where my health was going.

On the last day there, I woke up to find a stuffed lion on my window-sill. It had a note attached: "Dear Darlene, I love you, and I ain't lion. Love, Elizabeth." How sweet and heartwarming for her to gift that to me. It meant the world, and I have always treasured it.

I lost touch with her eventually, and I don't have her last name. I want to go back someday to show them their work, me. To say thank you again from the bottom of my heart.

TIE A YELLOW RIBBON

Thirty-one days of smiley face stickers on our calendars, and I was finally going home. When Elizabeth gave me the good news, I called my husband and told him to hurry over! Mom suggested they keep the good news from the kids, just in case I wasn't released. A very good point.

My grandmother and grandfather, who lived in the basement of mom's house, came up to wait for my return. Grandma said she was holding vigil until "Dolly came home" and didn't venture out until then. Although I was weak and had a long road to recovery, the thought of going home and seeing my babies reenergized me.

Turning down our block sent shivers down my spine and my eyes welled up. I could see yellow ribbons tied to our trees, blowing in the breeze, and a huge welcome home sign. It touched me beyond words. They were referencing the song by Tony Orlando, "Tie A Yellow Ribbon," and I knew immediately that it was my 'Welcome Home.'

I rang the bell and heard mom say to the kids, "Who could that be? Let's go see."

She opened the door, and when I walked in, I went to my knees and opened my arms. The kids came running, and we embraced. I was elated to be home. I kissed grandma, grandpa, and mom too.

Many years later, Jacquelyn told me that I smelled strange that day. Not like hairspray and perfume, but like the stale smell of a hospital. She got that right! But Dorothy from the Wizard of Oz was right too—"There's no place like home."

I began my recovery in a place I wanted to be more than anywhere else. I was home.

A SANITARY ROOM

My husband was a quiet wreck. He watched a tape the hospital gave him of how important it was to keep me as far away from germs as possible. My environment was supposed to be clean and dust free. Not many visitors, and they had to wear a mask.

While I was still at St. Agnes, he took the liberty of turning our kids playroom into a sanitary room for me. He painted the walls. Put in a bed, table, and TV. He took out all the dolls, cars, and games to make room for my stuff. New sheets and pillows. He showed me the room and was proud of it. I was so grateful for his thoughtfulness and hard work, but oh so sad that he wanted to keep me away from the one thing I wanted the most—our kids. He was adamant about the arrangements, however, so I complied.

Just a floor below, I lay in a hygienic bed with my clean sheets and germ-free air, listening to their tiny voices and little footsteps. I longed to be with them. I waited three rough weeks to be home, and I might as well have not been there at all. I didn't want to offend him, but this was torture.

I waited as long as I could, then slowly walked up the steps to be with them. They were asleep, and John was angry that I was there. He wanted me to rest and heal, but I wanted to be with my family. I don't remember how many nights I'd worked my way upstairs, but after a while, I never slept in the sanitary room again.

GOODBYE MASON REESE

Rest was my best friend now. Sleep was not only an escape, but the more I slept, the better I felt. Every day I felt stronger. Although it was a small amount of energy, it was moving in the right direction, even though I was bald, my eyes were sunk in, I'd lost weight, and could barely talk.

Waking up at times brought a few unwelcome surprises. I noticed on my chest wall a rash that had been steadily spreading and staining my skin. It was cellulitis, and I was put on antibiotics. I saw Dr. Ahmed on a regular schedule after the transplant. I had no strength to sit in the waiting room, though, so they had to put me in an empty examination room to lie down and wait until I was called.

Another scare one morning was a swollen face. I could hardly see my eyes. My sister and brother-in-law came over that day, and my brother-in-law said I looked like Mason Reese. He was right; I certainly did look like him. I just needed to find out why, so back to Westchester I went.

Elizabeth told me over the phone that all Dr. Ahmed would have to do is look at me and he'd know what was wrong, but I could hear the worry in her voice.

She was right, though. He walked in, quickly examined me, and said my catheter was blocked and it had to come out. He tried to remove it by simply pulling it out, but it was in there so long, my skin began to grow over the tubes. He tried pulling so hard, he stopped short at putting his leg on my chest to get more leverage. He told us I'd have to be admitted so they could surgically remove it.

In the end, I didn't have to stay. They gave me an open MRI, then nipped my skin, and the tube came out easily. Doctor told us he didn't want to keep me overnight because I had just gotten to go home, so he tried that instead, and it worked wonders.

By the time we drove back home, the swelling in my face had gone down considerably, and I was relieved that I didn't resemble a small child from '70s cereal commercials anymore.

ANGELS

Most of my intense treatments were over. I was getting stronger by the day and needed radiation therapy for six weeks.

My first visit was to get tattooed. Mom and the kids waited in the waiting room while I saw the technicians. They found the exact spots I needed the radiation to hit and the exact way I had to be positioned during the treatment.

The room I was in had big machines that, when turned on, made an unsettling loud noise. Each time I was put in the exact position as the day before, with my right arm over my head and twisted backward. It was not the most comfortable position, and it seemed like my arm would fall off just as the alarm sounded that it was over.

When I was set up each day and ready to go, they'd flip the lights off and the humming began. There was just enough light coming through where I could look up at the ceiling tiles and try to focus on one spot as I prayed.

I saw angel faces in the tiles. Every day, same three angels, same three spots for six weeks.

When it was all over, it turned out I needed an additional two more weeks of radiation, and by that time, I lost all the anxiety I had at the beginning.

I couldn't wait to meet with Dr. Gaynor again and see what he had to say about my health.

THE CROCHETED BLANKET: RECUPERATING

When I was feeling stronger, I would go sit with my mother and listen to the O.J. Simpson trial. At times, I would venture down to see my grandparents. I loved how they sat in complete silence in the middle of the afternoon. It was quiet and peaceful, yet I had company.

My husband had gone back to work, and the kids were in school.

I had a chill in my bones, and the only thing that kept me warm was my grandmother's crocheted blanket. I would rest on their sofa, and she would lay the blanket over me. I was comforted, warm, and safe. She'd also pull up a folding table and put a box of tissues near me.

When she cooked dinner, she'd call me into her kitchen and tell me to take a few nibbles. She made lentils in broth or pastina with milk and an egg—two things I felt I could swallow. My appetite was low and only she managed to get me to eat.

I would lie down and sleep until I heard the footsteps above me of the kids getting home. They'd run down to see me, and we'd all go upstairs to do homework and have a snack.

In 2001, at the age of 89, my grandfather began to have mini strokes. When confusion set in, I made sure he took his medications and made all of his doctor appointments, which I took him to as well. When he started having 'accidents,' I cleaned him up and made sure he never lost his dignity. He told me I was his nurse and that is how he coped. The decision was made to put him in a nursing home when things got intense, as I had two children under twelve that I tended to and could no longer care for him like he deserved. He was there but a few months when he passed away. Grandma Laura went into an understandable depression and shut down. I'd make my way from the attic to the basement, where they lived and give her breakfast and her medications. I took her to her doctor appointments and when she gave up self-care, I bathed her as well. I asked my mother to let her stay upstairs with her because she was very lonely and depressed. Mom agreed. When grandma couldn't sleep, mom would wake me up to sit with her. Mom expected me to hold it together and so I did.

Only a few short months after we lost grandpa Angelo, grandma Laura went to the hospital and died a few days later. Although she too was 89, I believe she died of a broken heart.

Grandma, your Dolly will love you and grandpa forever.

MUSIC TO MY EARS

Along with healing and reacclimating to being home again, I had a ton of mail and bills I had to look through. The bills were piling up, and no paychecks were coming in yet. John had just gone back to work after being home without pay for a month, so we had to play catch up, and it was overwhelming. Bill collectors were calling, and late payment notices were the majority of our mail.

In those days, the only thing I could do was to take my house phone off the hook to stop the madness.

Eventually, we got back on our feet.

Jacquelyn came home with a note from her teacher and asked for me to stop into the class for a visit when I was feeling better. I was looking forward to it and set up an appointment. I decided to bring the kids two dozen donuts, and when I walked in, the children got to their feet and applauded.

The teacher, Sister Diane, stepped aside as I searched the room for my girl. There she was, beaming with pride. My eyes burned with tears; her smile was the most beautiful thing I'd ever seen. We didn't take our eyes off each other.

The children rose from their seats and they began to sing "Jesus, Name Above All Names", in their angelic, sweet voices. It took my breath away. I had spent the past year fighting to be whole and healthy and present in my children's lives. Every heartbeat was a reminder that I was there, I was alive, and I was beyond thankful. The hymn was reaching into my soul and giving it a hug. As much as the medicine healed me, this moment lifted me up beyond what I thought was possible. I was loved and I loved them all right back. Time stopped and as I write this, I can picture each of them at their graduation many years later, and being so proud to know them all. They presented me with a huge Get Well card , each wrote something and signed their names. Whenever I come across it now, it takes me right back. I played that song on YouTube to remember the lyrics and if you can keep from tearing up, try and take a listen.

A LEMON GROWS IN QUEENS

A little worry wart was I. A tiny little thing with so many worries. A red spot on my arm, what could it be? A tummy ache, oh my, will I die? Everything scared me, and I was a bundle of nerves. Would there be a war and would the world the end? I wasted so of my life fretting over nothing because most of the things I feared never came true. I saw my mother worry about herself all of my life. She'd run up to her doctor if she saw him on the street. She'd make appointments about the slightest ache or pain. I saw that I probably should carry on like that as well.

Ironically, I stopped being so scared after my cancer diagnosis. From TMJ (a jaw problem when your mouth is not aligned), to breast cancer and a bone marrow transplant, from PMS to a radical hysterectomy, I've seen many an operating room.

Eighteen years after breast cancer, I tested positive for the BRAC gene. Dr. Gaynor sent me for a total hysterectomy, to be safe, to avoid getting ovarian cancer. I mentioned to my mother that she had a lemon—I was her lemon. She waved it off and said I was silly, but so much had happened to me, it was hard not to notice.

Off I went to have another surgery.

Everything went well. In fact, a robot performed the surgery while my surgeon was in control of it all. A week after, I was bored and did a little gardening to sit in the sun and recoup.

Looking back, that wasn't one of my best ideas. Because I had exerted myself, I began to hemorrhage.

I called the doctor, and she sent me to the ER. I reach out to my husband in the Bronx, and he left work, told me he'd meet me at the hospital. Our house is a half hour from the hospital, and he's one hour away.

The ambulance and my husband got there at the same time. Speed demon, no—well, yes. Nervous husband, definitely.

When the EMT guys opened the back doors to the ambulance, I heard my husband's voice. It was like angels singing.

My vitals were good in the ambulance, and I didn't lose consciousness. I was afraid I would slip into a coma because I was losing too much blood, but somehow, I managed to stay conscious.

The only gynecologist was on another floor delivering a baby. My husband looked worried but didn't vocalize it. Boy, there's never a dull moment being married to me. I had to give him credit for sticking to his vows through sickness and in health. He was an amazing trooper.

After waiting nine hours, I finally saw the gynecologist. She said one of the stitches had opened, and that was why I was bleeding.

That night, John drove me back to Teaneck, NJ to be admitted and have the doctor take care of the issue. She kept a close eye on me after I left the hospital, and I promised to rest in the meantime.

NINE ELEVEN

Back to school was in full swing as hair was combed, teeth brushed, breakfast eaten, bookbags placed on shoulders, and lunch boxes were full and ready to go. I dropped the kids off at school and went back home to do the usual daily things. John was home that day with a cold, and we sat to have breakfast while the TV was on in the background.

The show was interrupted by a scene of an airplane sticking out of the World Trade Center's North Tower. There was smoke and the brightest blue sky you could imagine. We froze as we watched. So much had gone through my mind. No way that was an accident. It was too clear outside, and the plane was way too low.

So much speculation and panicked reporting.

As we sat in awe and confusion, seven minutes later, we witnessed another plane flying quickly into view, lost sight of it, only for it to reappear and hit the South Tower. I was standing at the time, and my knees went weak. I sat on the sofa and began to cry.

We were shocked and overwhelmed.

I called the school to see if I could pick up the kids, but we were told that they were safe and to come at the regular time to get them. From where the school is located, the New York skyline was visible. The teachers were instructed to close the blinds and go on with their lessons.

My brother, Joe, was working in Manhattan that day, and I was a wreck. I called him and begged him to come home. I was shaking and couldn't wait to go pick the kids up.

The time had come, and I drove to the school. My daughter came out looking worried. My son was carrying on, not aware of what had happened. She got in the car and told me a classmate had on earbuds and heard the news and told all of her friends. She then explained it to her brother. I told her we were safe and took them home and made sure they watched a video instead of the never-ending recaps and visuals of that tragic day.

SUPER SANDY

Fall, my favorite time of year. Halloween, Thanksgiving, and Christmas. Sweater weather, cozy socks, warm fires, baking, and a roast in the oven.

October 2012, my Halloween decorations were up, inside and out, and I was preparing to buy the candy for the trick or treaters. There was talk about a storm coming and the possibility that we would have to evacuate. I decided not to go. Although I always took the advice of authorities, this time, I would stay.

The year before, we were introduced to Hurricane Irene. There was a mandatory evacuation, so the prep work began. Tables sat high up on the sofas. Furniture were brought to the upper floors because we lived in the basement apartment of my parent's house. John taped all the windows and put guards around them. We did everything to keep our things safe and left to stay with my brother, Joe. He lived further out on Long Island, and as the storm hit, we felt safe and secure at his house.

The next day, although we survived, trees were down everywhere. The news showed the destruction in each town, and people told their stories to the reporters. Everything settled down eventually, though, and we headed home.

The house and contents were as we left them. John removed the tape from the windows, placed the furniture back in their places, let the cats back out of their carriers, and we carried on.

Fast forward, October 2012, there was a severe storm on the horizon. The news was alarming, as usual, warning us to evacuate within the next two days. It was going to be big. The storm of the century. Quite scary, for sure. But did we want to batten down the hatches again and pack us all up and leave our home? Not really. Not this time.

We live in an area where we've been very fortunate not to have had any major weather destroy our property, so we felt safe, but you couldn't get away from the warnings, so even I was beginning to reconsider.

We do live in between the ocean and the bay. Something to think about.

John began taping the windows and took in all the outdoor patio furniture. There were news trucks riding around our city as the storm got closer to hitting. We had a mandatory evacuation warning, and they were coming around with bullhorns, directing us to leave. So, of course, we gave in, packed our things, and went to my brother Joe's again.

We hunkered down and were grateful to have the shelter of a loving family member who took all six of us in again, plus our cats. I felt completely at home there and never as though we were in his way at any time. No damage happened to his house, nor any houses nearby except for fallen trees.

We heard that our little city was hit hard, however, and it wasn't good. The streets were flooded, no electricity, no plumbing, no nothing. It was the deadliest, most destructive storm of the Atlantic in hurricane season.

Driving through town was a devastation to behold. Boats were thrown like they were discarded toys. Cars were juxta-positioned on streets and sidewalks, trees, garbage cans, and debris everywhere. It was the end of the world. It was eerie and depressing. There was a stillness and a flatness. Too shocked to react and too numb to cry.

Turning the key and opening up the front door gave me hope. Everything inside out house looked normal upstairs in mom's apartment. No water damage, no broken windows, nor fallen trees outside. A sigh of relief. Then, for our apartment.

We headed down. John was in front of me with a flashlight.

"Jesus Christ!" he shouted. "Stay there."

I stopped in my tracks. I almost didn't want to know. "What is it?" I asked finally.

He turned to me, looking crushed. "Everything is under water, at least four feet. Our furniture is floating around the room."

We lost it all. The photo albums and videotapes of our wedding and children growing up were the hardest to lose. We did what we could, then went back to my brother's house for three weeks.

Every day, John would take a trip home to clean up little by little. The town was shut down, no one in the streets, and only utility trucks and ambulances were hurrying about. There was a curfew, and when it got dark, without street lights, you couldn't see your hand in front of your face.

No one was allowed on the streets.

Eventually our lights came back, and so did our electricity. We moved back home, and mom and dad resumed their life as usual. All our furniture was in a huge heap at our curb, along with every neighbor on every block. We moved into the attic as the basement was being dried out and rebuilt.

On February 3rd, after spending the holidays cleaning up, we moved back into the basement.

John had developed COPD from breathing in sewage. He was forced to quit smoking. A habit that began when he was ten years old had come to an abrupt stop. It was a choice of either breathing or not breathing, so he gave up cigarettes.

Back to normal, at least for a while.

Eight years later, a pandemic would hit and a fire would come calling. It was 2020, and a nightmare was upon the entire world.

THE FIRE

My early sixties were sure to bring me peace and quiet, and a little house on the beach with less cooking and more enjoying my life.

Not so fast.

It was a rainy afternoon on October 12th, 2020. I was talking to my daughter, everyone was home, except my husband. I was at my favorite spot in the house, my desk, and Jacquelyn stood in front of me, chatting about this and that when we heard a crackling. We stopped talking. Listened. But it stopped. Nothing.

It happened again soon after, louder and more urgently. Crackling, sparking, electric. That was not the sound of anything remotely safe. On instinct, we ran outside and called to the others. We were already safely outside when flames came out of the side of the house. It was raining, and I had on pajamas and slippers. I ushered my parents into our neighbor's house after ringing their bell.

The fire department was called, and no sooner had we hung up, we heard the engines howling toward us. The block was filled with fire trucks and inspectors, as well as detectives and a fire chef. Neighbors gathered around and looked on.

Soaked from the rain, with slippers on, I saw my parents safely inside our neighbor's home when my son whispered that the cats were still inside the house. Panic shot up in me, and I alerted the chief. They had a hard time locating them and asked specifically where they might find them all.

Potato was the easiest, and they brought him to me. Chai was found, nervous, but not hurt. My daughter's cat, Luna, was in the worst shape. She was in the attic where the fire was headed and with all the smoke. Poor girl was foaming at the mouth when they found her. She was rushed to an awaiting ambulance and given oxygen.

She is well, and so are the other cats, I'm happy to say.

We stayed in a hotel that night, and it was a month before we found a rental. Our belongings were in storage. All two hundred boxes.

First day at the hotel, John and I left to go pick up some food, and while walking up the steps, he slipped and his arm twisted around as he tried to grab for the railing. It turns out, after MRI's and x-rays, he had a really bad tear in his rotary cuff. Surgery was recommended. And that would take another year because he had to get his A1C down because he had diabetes.

After a month at the hotel, we went into a rental for eight months, then had to move yet again because the house was sold. Imagine being in your early sixties, taking care of your elderly, ill parents, and not only moving all your stuff but theirs as well. We were beyond tired.

Covid was in full swing, too, and we were also quarantining before a vaccine was available.

The fourth move would come just four short months later. We moved back into our house. It was full of dust and not completed, but we were told we could move back in, and that was another nightmare. The contractors still had work to do. There were messes everywhere, and our two hundred boxes were ready to be dropped off. With no one to help us, we had to tackle it one day at a time.

And one day at a time was how it got done.

The house still needs work, but we're doing the best we can with all our individual aliments. I, with fibromyalgia, and John, with his bad shoulder, chronic back pain, two heart attacks, and diabetes, we're trudging along.

John and I had many scares with his health over the last few years. The first time he was having a heart attack, we did not recognize it as one. But after he began vomiting, I called 911. Still, I was surprised when the doctor told us it was indeed a heart attack. He seemed to heal quickly and was doing well when one evening he said he felt sick and I immediately felt concern. As the night wore on, he was not improving. It turned out to be a clogged stent and it had to be replaced.

To watch him suffer time and again, it scared me to think I might lose him. We bought bicycles and took rides around the neighborhood. One evening on our ride, my fender was making a noise and he turned around to see why. He fell off and landed on his handle bars. He said he had pain but we got back on our bikes and rode on.

As the night wore on, the pain increased, so the next day we went to Urgent Care. They took an x-ray but found no broken ribs. He suggested we go to the ER for further testing. The results were that his ribs were bruised and he should rest for a while to heal which took weeks.

In the meantime, I caught RSV and had a cough that was from hell. No fever, or sore throat though. I went to get tested and was given antibiotics. I was worried about John catching it with COPD and bruised ribs. His pain was getting worse instead of better but now he found it hard to breathe. Back to the ER we went.

Another x-ray showed he had double pneumonia. He was treated and released. It took a long time to recover and he had RSV to top it all off. We had a three day vacation coming up and we could not cancel. We went away on the back end of his illness and were determined to enjoy it. For the most part, it was nice, but recovering from an illness is not a great time to go on vacation. Despite all as my husband has been through, he keeps going and tries not to let it get him down. I, on the other hand, worry about him all the time.

Fire 2020

LOSING YOU

Everything was falling apart for us. Literally and figuratively. If someone were to tell me many of the things that were to come, I would certainly picture myself falling to pieces. But through all the turmoil, John and I put one foot in front of the other, almost robotically, and handled each situation as it came.

More was to come.

I started noticing subtle little things in my mother that didn't seem quite right. For example, when she had company at the dining table, she sat quiet, while in the past, she used to be at her happiest when surrounded by family and friends. She would talk and laugh and engage in conversations. Now, though, she sat quietly at the end of the table, where she always sat.

I lived downstairs and often came up to sit and say hello for a bit. She started asking me "What's up?" over and over again.

At first, I said to her "Why are you asking me every minute?" But she'd shrug and I let it go.

I continued to notice that she was off afterward, though. My daughter, Jacquelyn told me to take her to a doctor, and I made the appointment. She was examined, analyzed, and diagnosed with Alzheimer's. It was a devastating blow to the whole family.

We decided not to tell her or my dad. We went home and tried to live as normal a life as we could. Dad was retired, and they'd go for car rides and out to lunch or dinner. She stopped cooking and announced that she too was retired. She deserved to quit something she never enjoyed doing in the first place but dutifully did every single day of her married life. She eventually became incontinent, and we soon realized I had to take care of her personal needs.

Having fibromyalgia, this task was a brutal one. Just the trip up to her bedroom from the basement was hard.

Her bed was like an abandoned toilet. I couldn't clean it up. It was too much. But what could I do? Dad laid right next to her and never complained or noticed that he was lying in a pool of urine. Hiring a house cleaner wasn't the answer, either. We did, but eventually, she quit—and who could blame her.

Afterward, my brother hired a nurse. She came in four hours a day, which was a Godsend.

One afternoon, my parents took a ride in the car, but this time they weren't coming home. It was dark, and I was worried. Mom was still lucid and could operate her cell phone, which was a blessing. When I called, she said they were lost. I notified my brother, Joe, and he tried to direct them home, but dad was too confused.

After many hours, they pulled into a gas station, and Joe spoke to the attendant. He found out what town they were in and drove to get them. His husband, David, drove the car back and they reached our house about 3:00 a.m. Dad walked in like it was two o'clock in the afternoon. The time or the experience of getting lost for seven hours had no effect on him or mom.

That was the last straw for his driving.

Joe and I took away his keys. We were concerned he'd put up a fight or argue, so in the beginning, we told him the car wasn't working while I hid his keys.

Every day, he asked for them. And every day, I lied.

He eventually called Joe and said, "I want my fucking keys. I'm not a baby."

Joe would lie and reply, "As soon as the car is fixed, dad."

We kept doing this until he eventually stopped asking. I then became their official driver.

I took them to all their doctor appointments. I held onto their insurance cards and IDs. I made lists of all their medications. Made phone calls and took over their bills. Mom stopped cleaning the house and no longer maintained anything in it. And dad, well, it was harder to determine if he was ill too because he normally had a bad memory and spoke without a filter, but there came a time when my daughter again told me to get him checked.

He was diagnosed with Alzheimer's too.

The progression was slow, and as I write this, mom is eighty-seven and basically doing very well, aside from the incontinence and memory loss. She can hold a normal conversation and still loves company coming over. She's not bedridden and remembers us all. She's sweet and kind and agreeable.

Dad was a little harder. As I said, he had no filter, and things got intense occasionally. Dad would scream at me, "Get the fuck out of my house!" He said things like, "I don't like you anymore," and the ever popular, "Who the fuck do you think you are?" Sometimes his words hurt. I knew what I was dealing with, but it still hurt.

Some nights, as I was putting him to bed, he would try to throw a punch at me. Forever the boxer, his fist was closed and he threw his arm back, ready to land a right hook. I'd jump back and defused the situation by offering a cookie, which he took with a glass of milk.

"Thank you," he'd say.

"You're welcome, dad."

Losing them but having them right in front of me was the hardest part for me. I came from a position of being the third of their four children. I kept my place and had many authority figures above me. My parents, my grandparents, sister and older brother. I was quiet for a reason. No one heard me, everyone talked over me. I had no say, and when you have no say, you quickly learn to fall into the background. As I got older, I found my voice, but not knowing how to be heard, I went about it all wrong. I was then known for being a loudmouth. By starting to stick up for myself and being seen as brave or strong, I was looked at as too sensitive. I held that place all my life until there was no one home but me to take care of my parents.

It was difficult navigating my new position. I had to dictate when they would shower, eat, change their clothes, what to feed them, and spoon feed their medicine. After a while, I had to hand feed dad all his meals. Still, he would yell at me to stop.

I had to fool him into opening his mouth. I learned a few tricks here and there, and even stopped feeling bad when he cursed me. He was not well. He was in a lot of pain and suffering and had cataracts, which caused blindness because he was too weak to have the surgery. His weight plummeted to 95 lbs., and it could have been lower; we stopped weighing him because he couldn't stand up.

He was self-reliant all of his life. Loved and took care of mom and the four of us kids. It hurt my heart to watch him die before my eyes. He had the will to live, the fight was always in him. Many times, we'd wake up in the middle of the night with him screaming, "Help!" only to find him lying on the floor somewhere in the house, trying to get to the bathroom.

Family. That word means something very different than it used to for me. It used to mean a bunch of people you're related to. Now it means my kin, my heart, my responsibility. I will never walk away from a part of my heart.

I've seen life, and I've seen death. People I love have died, and I was near that door myself. It's a part of life that we will all reach one day. I want to reach that door knowing I loved well and took care of my own, and that I had integrity and did the right thing when I was called to do so.

MY LAST NAME IS FU....SCO

On May 23rd, 2022 my dad passed away. He was in the ICU, and maybe I'm an optimist or just stupid to think he was going to be okay. So many times he went to the hospital, and each time, he came back home to us. I know he was weak and losing weight. He was trying to be strong and tried hard to fight all the things that were breaking him down. He never lost his fighting spirit or his desire to help. If I was doing something in front of him, he would ask if he could help. Although I knew he couldn't, I smiled to myself. He always wanted to lend a hand.

It was getting harder and harder to care for him in that state. I had no idea what I was going to do and how long could I do it for. I just knew it was a day-to-day process. I had to try to get him to eat, to stay hydrated, to use the bathroom, to shower. All the normal things we do every day that we take for granted. Simple things like brushing our teeth or washing our hair. He couldn't do those things anymore.

Dad and Mom

Alzheimer's is a rough progression that, for the people witnessing it on a daily basis, breaks you down. I looked up to this man all my life. So strong and confident. So kind and sweet. There isn't anything he wouldn't do for us. He never asked for help, and there he was, helpless.

It was just John and I for the most part. We tried, but when you're called, and it's time to go, no one can keep you here.

I miss the sound of his voice. I miss how he'd ask for ice cream or bagels and lox. Chocolate was his favorite. Right before he went to bed, it was an Oreo cookie and glass of cold milk. I miss the smell of his cigar and the sound of boxing on TV. I miss rolling my eyes when he'd spell his name to strangers. "FU....sco," Not only would he get a good laugh from others, he laughed too, every time. I miss hearing my mom and dad sing. And the sound of an old movie playing in the background.

I see the empty seat next to mom now and the sadness in her eyes. Life is hard. You work and struggle. Then you grow old, and things slow down. We get those little moments where something makes us happy, and it's in those moments that make life worthwhile.

We should all do more of the things that bring us joy, no matter how small. Those are the times in life that we'll remember. Those are the things that mean love.

The night before he passed, I was at a baptism. I left early to go see him. As I was driving, I thought of going home to shower and get comfortable. I thought, maybe I'll just go tomorrow. I got a little lost, and it was getting late, yet I found myself driving into the hospital parking lot and getting out of the car regardless.

He was in the ICU, and it was a long walk through the corridors. When the nurse saw me enter, she said, "Who is Joan?"

I said, "She's my mother."

She smiled softly. "He keeps calling for her."

I went to his bedside and saw that they had a bubble blanket on him. It looked like foam and it was puffy. He was cold, and maybe that's why they gave it to him.

I told him I was there and said, "I love you."

He said, "I love you too."

That's something that was never said in our house, so it felt funny saying it, but it also felt good. It wasn't the first time I told him that, though. I told him many times during the time I cared for him.

When he spoke, he sounded weak, almost desperate. His voice was shaky, and his face and body twitched. I began to cry and couldn't stop. I asked the nurse why he was twitching, but she didn't tell me. Now I think I know.

I held his hand and covered him, just like he liked me to do at home. Sheets all the way up under his neck. His toes tucked in.

He said, "Joanie, oh how I wish I could hear your voice, just one more time."

I squeezed his hand. "I love you, Carlo." I knew, that's all he wanted. I sound very much like mom, and I gave him his last wish. Then I kissed his forehead and left.

The next day, I called the hospital in the afternoon because the doctor usually called me with updates, but I hadn't heard from him. The nurse put me on hold and when she came back, she just blurted out that he passed.

"Excuse me? What? Did you say he passed?"

"Oh, yes. I'm so sorry," she said.

It took me by surprise. Why did I think he would be okay? Maybe that's why I couldn't stop crying the night before. Deep down, I knew he was shutting down. Deep down, I knew I would never see him alive again.

John and I went to pay our last visit to dad, who was still in the ICU. His cubby curtain was shut, and we made our way inside. Everyone gave their condolences as we walked passed them.

Mom receiving Dad's veterans flag

There was a lump in my throat as I walked up to him. I touched his face. It was as cold as ice and hard like stone. I covered him again, right up to his neck, but his toes were sticking out.

I looked at John, who was at the foot of his bed. "Can you cover his feet?"

"Really?" He asked.

"Yes. Really."

We talked to him and told him we'd take good care of mom, told him to go be with his brothers and his mom and dad.

It was one of the hardest days of my life.

He had a veteran's funeral. He was honored and mom was presented with the American flag that we showcase on our mantel. He was going to be ninety-two years old in July.

Bless you, dear dad. For as long as I live, I will miss you.

A NEW NORMAL

Life after cancer began a new normal. Life after 9/11 and the fire brought another new normal. We never know what the future will hold, and it's a blessing that we don't. Just anticipating what may happen will send anyone into a tailspin of anxiety.

We have to hope for the best, do our best, and be there are peaceful moments that we can rest, re-energize, and regroup.

Starting to live my life again after cancer was filled with a wonderful sense of tranquility and gratitude. I found myself having a difficult time going back to the hair salon for a trim, not due to the fact that they would cut my hair or that it was the same place they shaved my head. No, it was the human touch. So many doctors, nurses, and technicians had fussed and poked at me for so long, anyone who touched me automatically made me tremble.

As she grabbed a piece of my hair and held it up between her fingers, my eyes welled. I had to control the urge to sob. Again, John was by my side, consoling me and having my back.

That passed after a time, and most of my PTSD and anxiety went with it.

I look forward to the little things in life. They're more frequent and joyful than the big moments. I enjoy gardening, reading, watching a TV show with my husband and the kids when they're home. I like to write and do crafts. I have an Etsy shop called Treasure Door, where I make birdhouses, bookshelf book sitters, wire dolls, and plaques. And of course, I love to write.

I'm so thankful to have had the honor of watching my kids grow and become wonderful people. My husband and I just celebrated our 38th wedding anniversary, and now we've been together forty-six years in total. He was my rock and my strength while I was ill, and he's been by my side through the good and not so good.

Family is everything to me, and without them, I don't know if I would have survived.

Life is good, even in turmoil. You have your people beside you to get through to the good stuff. It's the Yin and Yang, the duality that makes you appreciate and have gratitude.

ACKNOWLEDGMENTS

In addition to the people I mentioned above, there are people who I need to acknowledge and thank for their part in my journey.

I want to thank my oncologist, Dr. Mitchell Gaynor. He was the reason I survived. He was one of the best doctors on the planet and one of the kindest, most empathic doctors. Truly one of a kind. I only wish every doctor was as knowledgeable, gentle, and kind as he was to his patients. He passed away several years ago, and I'll always miss him.

I also appreciate every doctor, nurse, and technician that's cared for me, from the simplest procedure to the most intricate.

Dr. Ahmed made the hardest part of my treatments something I can look back on and realize what precise and exact science it takes to treat someone receiving a bone marrow transplant. I could have had so many setbacks, but I didn't because he was that good. I felt so completely loved by all of them. As if I was placed in the palm of their hands and gently turned over to the next until I was healed, cured, and freed.

I was set free, back into the world to live my best life. I was taught a lesson of the human spirit. I will never wish those memories away, not even the darkest days that too have a place in my heart.

Without my younger brother, Joseph, I would have never had the good fortune to be treated by Dr. Gaynor, and this all would have had a much different ending. Joseph literally took me by the hand those first few days and saw my husband and I through every test I had to take and all the running back and forth to Manhattan. He bought me vitamins, set up a schedule for me to take them, told me what I should be eating, and made me drink shark cartilage believe it or not.

It was said that sharks don't get cancer, so he bought me a few bottles, and I had to hold three drops under my tongue for a few seconds before swallowing it. It tasted like toilet water, but at that point, I would do anything to be healthy. He is my hero.

My parents were right there by my side at every point. Always with me, driving me to office visits, watching the kids when I went for chemo, doing my laundry while I was away for three weeks, cooking for my family, and loving me through my illness. Everyone went through my cancer ordeal with me and suffered too. I'm a lucky girl to have so much love and support.

I don't know how I would have been driven to survive if I wasn't a mother. Every cell in my body didn't want to leave my children. I imagined how it would be for them growing up without me. Who would help John raise them? How different would they be as people without me? I never wanted the answers to those questions. I wanted to raise them. I wanted to watch them grow up, and I wanted to be there whenever they needed me, no matter how big or small, how silly or serious. I'm overwhelmingly grateful that I survived my illness to watch them become who they are today.

Lastly, my husband, who was everything to me, especially during those hard times. He gave me shots for two days in a row after every chemo. He cleaned my catheter tubes every night. He took days off to drive me to chemo, stayed with me during it, and took me home. He watched the kids, took them fishing, and cleaned the house. He was supportive and loving, and I appreciated it all.

Marriage is sometimes hard and even more challenging with an illness. Things can get messy and stressful. That's why I'm grateful for all he did for us. He showed up when things got scary and stayed there.

So, buckle up for the ride of a lifetime. Make plans and watch them not happen. Take what is handed to you and go with it. Somehow, we make it through.

There are lessons in the hard times that make us stronger, build character, and teach us to appreciate the good times.

Thanks for reading my story.

ABOUT THE AUTHOR

Darlene Fusco Weinbrenner was born in Manhattan, New York. She currently resides on Long Island, NY with her husband, John, son, John, mother, Joan, and cat, Potato.

As a writer, Darlene enjoys sharing her life experiences and the growth that came from each adversity. Family is most important to her.

Darlene's voyage through life, so far, has had many ups and downs which taught her invaluable lessons including, patience, strength, and empathy. Her strategy for the darkest times has been to simply "put one foot in front of the next and follow a path out of the darkness." If you are looking for hope, resilience, or wondering how to keep going, there is a message in her story.

www.ingramcontent.com/pod-product-compliance
Lightning Source LLC
Chambersburg PA
CBHW061156120626
46546CB00005B/2084